"I'M NOT A WOMEN'S LIBBER, *But..."*

Anne Bowen Follis

foreword by Lynda Johnson Robb

"I'M NOT A WOMEN'S LIBBER, But..."

and other confessions of a Christian feminist

ABINGDON
NASHVILLE

"I'M NOT A WOMEN'S LIBBER, BUT . . ."
AND OTHER CONFESSIONS OF A CHRISTIAN FEMINIST

Copyright © 1981 by Abingdon

Library of Congress Cataloging in Publication Data

FOLLIS, ANNE BOWEN, 1947–
    I'm not a women's libber, but— and other confessions of a Christian
feminist.
    1. Feminism—United States. 2. Women's rights—United States.
    3. Housewives—United States. 4. Christian life—1960–
    I. Title.
    HQ1426.F75   305.4'2   81-1241   AACR2

ISBN 0-687-18687-0

Scripture quotations unless otherwise noted are from the Revised Standard
Version of the Bible, copyrighted 1946, 1952, 1971, © 1973, by the Division
of Christian Education of the National Council of the Churches of Christ in
the U.S.A., and used by permission.

Quotations noted TEV are from the Bible in Today's English Version.
Copyright © American Bible Society 1966, 1971, 1976.

Quotations noted NIV are from The New International Version, New
Testament. Copyright © 1973 by The New York Bible Society International.
Used by permission.

MANUFACTURED BY THE PARTHENON PRESS AT
NASHVILLE, TENNESSEE, UNITED STATES OF AMERICA

To my husband Dean,
who has been my sharpest critic and my staunchest supporter;
my sounding board and my "devil's advocate"; my partner
and my friend;

To my parents,
Donald and Leona Hotaling Bowen, who taught me years ago
that life is worth very little if one is not willing to struggle to
find answers, and to stand by what is right;

To Troy, Ryan, and Megan,
who bring my life endless delight, diversions, frustrations,
surprises, and joy.

Contents

Foreword

The scene was the national convention of the National Women's Political Caucus. The time was about one month after I had assumed the Chair of the President's Advisory Committee for Women, and this was my first opportunity to speak before the leadership of the organized women's movement. I knew I was being looked over very carefully, and I was nervous.

The occasion was a luncheon celebrating the Equal Rights Amendment and several leaders in the struggle for ERA ratification had been invited to speak. And while I was sitting there, mentally biting my nails to the nub, a lively blond woman got up to speak. And when Anne Follis finished her eloquent remarks—punctuated several times by applause—she was greeted with a standing ovation. The reception she got fed my courage, not only because the audience was sympathetic, but also because what she said struck a very deep chord in my spirit.

The sympathy of that audience not only made it

easier for me to speak, but it also represented something critically important. That is, I believe, one of the major points Anne is making in this important book: those women, among the leading feminists in this country, understand and share the belief that when they talk about equality for women, they are talking about *all* women—women who work inside the home as well as those who work outside.

That day Anne gave me my HERA (Homemakers' Equal Rights Association) button. "Every mother is a working mother" it proudly declares. This book clearly points out that homemakers deserve—and require—the same kind of rights that women working outside the home do.

The President's Advisory Committee for Women traveled across the country to hear what American women were thinking and feeling about their lives, and we learned that those who say that the women's movement represents only a small number of people are wrong. There is another—growing—movement of women who are willing and able to understand that they are being discriminated against solely because of their gender, and they are ready to speak out about it.

We heard from widows who discovered when it was too late that they were not covered by their husband's pension benefits. We spoke with former military wives, who, after a lifetime of military service received a "dishonorable discharge" through divorce, and were left with no benefits and no skills that could be translated into a civilian job. We heard from homemakers whose Social Security benefits were totally inadequate because they had never been employed. And they have all learned that equality and justice for them does not mean giving up anything, or being forced to do anything against their will, but that it means gaining independence, and the luxury, if you will, of being homemakers to the fullest extent.

My time at the Advisory Committee has been a great learning experience for me in many ways. I came to my job as a strong supporter of the Equal Rights Amendment, feeling that it is the last great piece of human rights legislation left undone by this country. I have learned, though, that there are many other issues affecting the homemaker, the infant, the student, the teacher, the worker, that require action for positive change. That is why this is an important book for every woman to read. Over and over again, Anne Follis makes the point that those changes we are seeking are life-enhancing, family-enhancing, and spirit-enhancing.

Anne Follis and I have much in common. Despite the fact that I grew up in the public eye, when I graduated from college I felt that what I wanted most to do was marry, care for my children, and manage my household. Clearly that has paid off in the richness of my life with my husband and my children. Like Anne, I have come to understand it is that richness which makes it possible and necessary for me to work for full equality for women. For women and men were created equal by God, and must become so in the eyes of the law of this land.

Lynda Johnson Robb

1

"I DON'T
NEED TO BE
LIBERATED"

It was five-thirty in the
evening, the worst time of the day for the phone to
be ringing. At five-thirty I am usually preparing
dinner, the cue for the kids to, as my mother puts it,
"zero in for the kill."

On the other end was a long distance call from a
man who was writing a newspaper column on
women's rights. Did I have a minute? He'd like to
ask me a few questions.

Did I have a minute? I thought as my four-year-old
swung around my legs, making noises like a truck. At
the same time the dog was licking the butter from the
table, and my seven-year-old was calling from down
the hall that he couldn't find his blue socks. (*Good
grief, what did he need them for now?*) Meanwhile,
my two-year-old had managed to get the refrigerator
door open, and was pulling food out with remarkable
speed, demanding in her little but persistent voice,
"Eat, Mommy! Eat, Mommy!" I asked the caller to
hold while I restored peace as best I could. When I
returned he began his questioning.

"First," he said, "I'd like to know if you're *really* a housewife."

The question, however ironic, was one I have become used to. There are certain stereotypes that are hard to break, and one of the most rigid is of the career-minded, secular feminist. Being a home-maker and a minister's wife, my involvement in the struggle for women's rights has seemed to many to be a contradiction in terms.

I understand the confusion all too well. In the years since the feminist movement began to invade my thinking I have been forced to deal with a great many questions and apparent contradictions myself.

After all, how does a Christian wife and mother cope with the twentieth-century women's move-ment? Books dealing with that question have been coming off the presses in the last decade with increasing frequency, many offering simplistic answers to what is a very complex question.

The question is a pertinent one for me because, as a Christian wife and mother, I have been drawn increasingly into the political struggle for women's rights. And for me, the simple answers didn't work.

In the early seventies I put aside a career as a secretary to have a baby and be a full-time wife and mother, something I had dreamed of doing most of my life. In addition, having had a rather dramatic conversion experience at a young age, my beliefs were intensely Christian and biblically based.

Steeped in these traditional values, the onset of the women's movement came as a jolt. Initially I reacted defensively. I remember telling a friend once, when asked my opinion of "this women's lib thing," "*I don't need to be liberated.*" But in spite of myself, a growing identification with many of the political and philosophical ideals of the feminist movement began to emerge. The result was an enormous personal conflict, as I tried to find my place amid an issue that was becoming increasingly polarized.

In 1973 I was asked if I'd be interested in attending a brunch for legislators in Springfield, Illinois— twenty miles away from where I was then living—on behalf of the proposed Equal Rights Amendment. It was a subject I knew little about, but it seemed reasonable to me, and I had been annoyed by what appeared to me to be the scare tactics of its opponents.

I went, and was soon active in efforts to promote the amendment in my district. I began studying the subject, lobbying, organizing, and speaking to groups. It was all very exciting, and I loved it, but my self-consciousness at being a part of what was by some jeeringly called "women's lib" was acute. In addition, I was a housewife, and suspected that as such I would never be regarded as a true and loyal feminist within the movement.

At the same time, I began to get letters and phone calls from people quoting the Bible in what was sometimes a desperate effort to get me to see the "error of my ways." (It was always presumed that I didn't know a thing about the Bible.) In my first debate my opponent declared, with an air of self-righteousness, that some "so-called religious people do support the Equal Rights Amendment, but *true* Christians, who believe that the Bible is the Word of God, oppose it." I began my reply by saying, "As one who believes that the Bible is the Word of God. . . ."

Of course, these pious judgments by a few small-minded people whom I didn't know were trivial, and in my own church I continued to feel loved and accepted. Nevertheless, I began to feel somewhat displaced. I was a Christian; my faith meant everything to me. Yet here I was, presumed by other Christians to be an outsider. That had never happened to me before, and it hurt.

The question for me, then, became not how to cope with the feminist movement per se, but how, as a Christian wife and mother, to cope with an emerging personal identification with feminism. And that is the subject of this book. While is not an autobiography, it is an account of the struggle of one person seeking to remain true to the Word of God and at the same time to recognize the realities of the world in which we live.

"I DON'T NEED TO BE LIBERATED"

I have become convinced that society's assumptions about the low value of women, reflected dramatically in our legal system (the term "second-class citizens" applies here) leave many women without an adequate sense of worth, or the confidence to carry out their chosen roles in a positive way. I realize that may sound rather trite and something of a cliché to people who are bored with the clamor for women's rights. But in the past few years I have met too many individual women who have personally been affected by legal and social injustices, and I have uncovered too many laws that demean women to continue to turn my back on a movement which is clamoring for fairness to women. Besides, "I don't need to be liberated" is very much its own cliché, bred out of a selfishness which says, "As long as things are OK with me, I don't care about women who are less fortunate." I can no longer abide that attitude in myself or ignore it in others.

And so, through what has often been a difficult personal conflict, I have begun to discover that the struggle to merge apparently contradictory beliefs does not have to be a threat to those beliefs; it can strengthen them. And it can bring about growth and adventure as well!

2
A NICE
GIRL LIKE ME

"What's a nice girl like you doing lobbying for the Equal Rights Amendment?"

The question was put to me by a legislator from what was then my district as we stood outside his office. I had never lobbied before, but a friend of a friend had told me about this ERA Day at the state capital. My one and only child was just a year old and, taking him with me, I went, more out of curiosity than anything else. As we stood in the hallway corridor my son was fighting desperately to be let down. "You see," the legislator continued, "you're caring for your baby and your husband's at work, and that's the way it should be." With that, the subject was closed.

An hour earlier I wasn't even sure I was *for* the Equal Rights Amendment. For that matter, I was so politically ignorant that I didn't know for certain who my legislators were, much less where they stood on the ERA. But that conversation marked a turning point in my life that I'll never forget.

Nice girl? Yes, I was the original "nice girl." I was

raised in a home that emphasized morals and integrity. We went to church on Sundays, and I was taught traditional values. My mother was an independent, knowledgeable woman, and a full-time homemaker. My father was a businessman who, I remember, always patiently took his three kids along when he went on errands and who seemed genuinely to enjoy his family. And what did I want to be when I grew up? A wife and mother. I might pursue some other career to "fall back on" just in case, but my goal in life was to be a homemaker. I was sure no other career could be as rewarding and worthwhile as being a full-time wife and mother.

That didn't change as I grew up. I met Dean when I was twenty, working in Philadelphia as a secretary. He was twenty-six and in the army at Fort Dix, New Jersey. We met on a blind date at a hymn sing in a Baptist church. I had been warned by some conservative friends that he was terribly "worldly," so I expected the worst. He had worked at various jobs all over the country, and had a dynamic, dominating personality. He exuded self-assurance, yet underneath there was evidence of a kind of vulnerability and of a very deep faith. On top of that, he wanted to be a *minister*. I thought he was wonderful.

Within a week I was photographed sitting on the

hood of his convertible. Years later I found those snapshots, and all I could think of was what a dummy I'd been, posing on the car like a stupid hood ornament! (An old friend of his recently remarked to me, "I can't believe Dean Follis married a feminist." I replied, "Believe me, he didn't!")

We were married six months after we met. Shortly after that he was out of the army and going to seminary in Chicago, pastoring at a little weekend church in the country. Finally, in 1970, he finished school and took his first full-time church. A year later I was able to quit working outside the home and settle down with our first child. I felt like I'd died and gone to heaven!

About that time the women's movement hit. I reacted to it with suspicion, if not outright defiance. "What do those women want, anyway?" I remember remarking to Dean as we watched a feminist protest on the television news. They all looked so . . . so . . . so *unladylike*. I felt quite smug and superior.

It was about then that I coined the phrase, "*I* don't need to be liberated." (Actually, I didn't coin the phrase at all. As I later discovered, countless other women were saying exactly the same thing, each believing the phrase to be original.) I was happy and secure in my traditional life, and I viewed the movement as a threat. All the talk about getting women out of the home and into the work force, which so dominated the movement in those days, made me uneasy and resentful.

But, in spite of myself, the emphases of the movement began to sink in. I laughed at an article by a woman who resented the fact that her doctor took all the credit for delivering her baby when, in fact, *she* had done all the work. I identified, from my own brief experience, with women in the business world who bemoaned the dead end, step-'n'-fetch-it jobs that were, invariably, assigned to women. Even as an executive secretary my job had offered no real opportunity for advancement, and included pouring coffee and running across the street for cigarettes. I had never been a victim of sexual harassment on the job, but I'd known women who had been. Although it angered me, I thought the only way to deal with it was to quit. Not until the ideals of the feminist movement began to invade my thinking did it occur to me that women might actually unite and fight these injustices.

The poster of Israel's Prime Minister Golda Meir, with the caption "But can she type?" really hit home. I had worked for a while in a personnel office and knew that women were treated differently than men when applying for a job, but for years I had just accepted it. It wasn't until the women's movement came along that I began to recognize the underlying presumption in all of this: that women are inferior people. High-sounding words about "pedestals" and the "flower of womanhood" no longer worked in disguising the unequal treatment—and regard—which society afforded its women.

Even in my own life, I began to recognize this attitude. I would rather work for a *man*; I wanted a *son*; I sat back, detached and uninvolved as my husband made major decisions affecting our family. I thought about the churches I'd been in, where men took the offering, lead the prayers, preached, ministered, and made most of the important decisions, while women taught the children's Sunday school, made coffee, and took notes at the meetings.

Before I knew it, my annoyance with the silly issues, like whether or not women should shave their legs or wear long dresses, began to give way to acute agreement with the more important ideals of equality. The more I read about the women's movement, the more I found myself saying, "That's so *true!*"

And I was angry. I thought of the vulgar remarks my high school friends and I had been subjected to when we'd walked past a building crew. I thought about the times I had played dumb, or submerged my own interests and talked about those of my date, in order to protect his ego. I thought about rape laws which forbade any mention of the rapist's criminal history in court, but allowed the dredging up of often distorted information about the victim's sexual past.

I began complaining about it all, until one day Dean told me to either *do* something, or stop talking. (As a minister he'd seen too many people who complained incessantly about what they didn't like, but were unwilling to get involved and do some of the work needed to make changes.) I took it as a challenge.

It was about that time that I heard, through channels, about the ERA event to be held at the state capital. I knew very little about the Equal Rights Amendment, and I didn't think it had any relevance for me as a homemaker. But I thought it was time I plunged ahead and got involved, so I packed some diapers and a jar of baby food for Troy and took off for Springfield.

As I read the material there on the Equal Rights Amendment it all made good sense to me. I heard someone remark that its opponents reminded her of "the same people who told us sex education would involve live demonstrations in the classroom." I had a good laugh and commented that I couldn't believe anyone would fall for their scary stories about co-ed toilets and communist plots.

We had a nice brunch and heard a few peppy speeches. I decided I should do something more. It was then that I went over to the capital building to have the conversation with my legislator. I had learned at an information table that he was against the amendment but, I thought, he's an elected official. His arguments will be reasonable, and he'll be open to what I have to say. I expected an intelligent conversation. I was completely unprepared for his patronizing, illogical attitude. More than anything, our discussion confirmed my support for the Equal Rights Amendment. I left Springfield determined to get involved.

But, of course, the issue was more than just the Equal Rights Amendment. By taking an active, and increasingly visible position on this issue, I was becoming aligned more and more with the feminist movement. Me. The one who had posed on the hood of a car and protested that I was above needing to be liberated. And, as much as I enjoyed the challenge and excitement of what I was doing, it raised questions about the values in my life like nothing I had done before.

There seemed to be so many contradictions. I was sure that the Equal Rights Amendment posed no threat to the homemaker, but I was afraid that it was the goal of the women's movement as a whole to obliterate her role. No one in the movement told me that, although there were a few feminists who seemed to be saying that in those days. But mostly I was hearing it from ERA opponents who were determined to discredit the Equal Rights Amendment by identifying it as part of a totally radical movement. Guilt-by-association? Yes! Right out of the pages of the McCarthy era! And even I fell for it at first.

I handled my fears by saying that the movement was about freedom to choose: allowing women to work in the home or outside of it with no stigma attached to either choice. Still, in my heart, as a full-fledged happy homemaker, I believed that the major benefits of the women's movement would be felt by career women who experienced discrimination in employment. But, studying the laws of various states relating to women, I began to realize that it was for the homemaker as well. I was stunned as I began to uncover examples of unfair laws which discriminate against married women by giving inordinate power to the husband in areas of property rights, or inheritance laws, or domicile laws. Since the homemaker is, of all people, the most vulnerable, because she has no income of her own and is entirely dependent on another for support, these laws undermine her position and threaten the very institution of the family itself.

As I traveled and spoke to larger audiences,

women began writing to me for help. I received pathetic letters from women who had been beaten by their husbands. One woman wrote a letter describing the years of abuse she had endured from a now dead husband, and the fear and helplessness she had felt. "People say to me now, 'Why didn't you just leave,'" she wrote to me. "But unless you've been in that situation you can't imagine the feeling of powerlessness and worthlessness. There was a part of me that honestly believed I *deserved* it all!"

Her letter was articulate and appealing. She concluded with a long list of her credits, including a college education and presidency of a statewide women's organization. She said, "I don't know why I'm telling you this, except that I feel I must prove my worth to people. I still feel that way."

Letters came from many women who were victims of a bitter divorce. I couldn't believe the number of letters I got from women whose problems were similar to the one who wrote: "I cooked for him, I cleaned for him, I entertained his business associates, I raised his kids. He wanted me to stay home, so I stayed home. Then he leaves, and the courts tell me that I get a *percent* of his property and earnings as a *favor*, but the bulk of it all belongs to him because he earned it. What do they think I *did* all those years?"

I soon discovered that the big divorce settlement where the wife takes her husband to the cleaners is the exception rather than the rule. Alimony is hard to get, and even child support is rarely enforced adequately. And the homemaker, who has no income of her own and often no skills or job experience (or what would qualify as job experience) is, invariably, hurt the most.

One woman wrote that when her husband died she had to pay five hundred dollars to go to court to prove that she didn't have to pay inheritance tax on their jointly owned business. "But if I had died, for him it would have been business as usual." Another wrote that, although separated from her husband, she didn't believe in divorce. As a result, "I can't vote; I can't run for public office; my daughter can't even go to the nearby state college on the rates of an in-state resident, because legally our domicile is with *him*. And he hasn't contributed a dime to our support in years!"

Some of the women wrote for help, and I tried to refer them to organizations that might provide some assistance. Sometimes I was able to and sometimes I wasn't.

A lot just wrote looking for a sympathetic ear. I listened, I wrote back, I prayed a lot, and sometimes I cried.

As I became more and more involved, I began to

27

realize that something was happening to me. There had been a comfortable complacency existing at an unconscious level in my life. In spite of my own resistance, it was giving way to an acutely conscious, deeply felt sense of compassion and awareness of injustice. My life had always been so secure, I had rarely taken seriously the problems of others less fortunate than myself. But now I was being confronted, face to face, with some terrible injustices and inequities. Social and legal inequities that suddenly seemed too great, and too close, to continue to ignore.

I can't be sure where it was, but somewhere along the line I reached a point where there was no turning back.

"BORN AGAIN"

The phone rang just as I was sitting down to lunch. "Could you get some of your people out to talk to Senator so-and-so this week?"

It was the ERA headquarters in Springfield. It seemed that some ERA opponents had set up in the capital for legislators to visit a display, which supposedly depicted the kind of people who support the Equal Rights Amendment. To describe the display as inflammatory and pornographic would be an understatement. Using guilt-by-association smear tactics, the display lifted quotes from various feminist leaders out of context; emphasized the most radical and controversial elements of the feminist movement; and posted homosexual material, stating that these were the people who *really* support the Equal Rights Amendment.

"We thought it was so obnoxious that it would only hurt the opposition rather than help them," the caller told me, "but, would you believe, it has actually weakened a few pro legislators?"

I was annoyed and disgusted, and not in the mood to have my day ruined by the news. "Who set this thing up, anyway?" I asked.

When she told me the name, it was not familiar. "Who is she?" I asked.

"Oh, you know," the caller told me, "she's one of those *born-again* Christians."

Her voice was so sarcastic and contemptuous when she said the words "born again" that I choked on my sandwich. When I regained my composure, I said somewhat timidly, "So am I."

She was shocked into an awkward silence. Born-again Christians, I could hear her thinking, are self-righteous, overbearing people. This Anne Follis is a friend of mine. What is she saying? She can't be one of *them*.

But I am. When the country first took notice of presidential candidate Jimmy Carter, one intriguing facet of the man was the fact that he called himself a born-again Christian. Many reacted to it almost as if it was some sort of a new fad. There seemed to be a new born-again celebrity every week. Books dealing with the phenomenon began appearing even in secular bookstores and at drug counters. Whatever it was, it was marketable, and before long a certain Madison Avenue element to the born-again craze made it almost cheap. At least, it seemed that way to me.

"Born again" was more than just a slick slogan to

put on a bumper sticker. For me it had been a precious, life-changing experience. And on the phone that day, as so many times since, I felt compelled to explain that, and to apologize for the excesses that are often associated with the experience.

It is possible to go to church all your life, and yet to grow up with a spiritual vacuum. Religion was secondary in my life as I went through high school and into college; what I wanted most was to find the right man, get married, and settle into a nice, comfortable, middle-class life. I wanted more than security, though. I wanted a loving relationship that would last a lifetime.

There was a certain hollowness in the friendships I acquired in those years. I couldn't quite put my finger on it, but I wanted more. Once, during a particularly lively class picnic I broke away from the festivities and went off into the woods alone. "I was looking for something," I wrote later in my diary, "but I don't know what it was, and I didn't find it." (I believe now that I was experiencing the gentle pull and tug of the Holy Spirit in my life.)

It didn't make sense, this vague yearning of mine. I had a good family, plenty of friends, and lots of things to keep me busy. But I wanted more. I convinced myself that when I finally found the right guy and fell in love, I would be happy.

The right guy took a while in coming along, and

something happened in the meantime. The young woman with the big, romantic fantasies was born again.

Volumes have been written to explain just what that means, and some of them are very good. Essentially, what it comes down to is an entering into an intimate relationship with God through Jesus Christ. I had come to recognize my own failures and needs and . . . I just wanted more *substance* in my life. And I found the love and the wholeness offered in Jesus Christ to be absolutely irresistible.

I didn't go forward to an altar and have an emotional breakthrough. It happened in the quiet of my room, as I was reading the Bible (a book to which I had paid little attention, and for which I had some disdain, in spite of my religious upbringing). All my life I had felt a little like I was on a treadmill, dealing with resentment, frustration, disappointment, and trying, trying, trying to do things "right"—only to discover as I got one hole in the dike plugged up that three more had burst. But that evening I turned to the fifth chapter of Galatians and read that when we allow human nature to rule our lives the treadmills will abound, but when the Spirit controls our lives, we will have "love, joy, peace. . . . Against such things there is no law" (NIV).

I remember a surge of relief and feeling downright gleeful! The old, overworked phrase about "letting go and letting God" became a reality in my life as I got off the awful treadmill of trying to manage my own life and let the Spirit of God enter and fill the void.

There are a few problems with testimonies such as I have just shared. For one, they tend to be easily overplayed. What Christ has done in my life in the years since this experience is actually far more significant. For another, they begin to sound a little bit alike after a while, and often end with the simplistic claim that "since then everything has been perfect in my life and I haven't had any problems." That claim, I suspect, is pure fiction. At least I can't make it.

No instant, dramatic changes occurred in my life. The changing and the growth have been slow, even painful at times. There have been struggles with my own confusion, my own doubts, and the frustrations of trying to live the Christian life amid the complexities of today's world. Immediately after my decision I found myself trying to work out my beliefs and define terms, and I studied the Bible as one who had just found water after being lost in the desert. I was constantly trying to relate my faith to the present day and to my own life. How is one to be "in" the world but not "of" it? Why is there so much evil, suffering, and pain in this world? Why do I continue to sin, to fail God, to live like the "old" me?

Sometimes the pieces fit, and sometimes they didn't. Gradually, however, the feeling of urgency to find the answers lessened. When, through prayer and study and struggle some new understanding would come it was great, but as I grew in my relationship with God I learned to trust him even with that which I could not yet understand.

And I discovered joy. Rich, abundant, glowing, charged-up joy. It came unexpectedly at first: while having my coffee in the morning, or reading a book, or watching TV, or driving the car, or sitting in church. I'd think about the greatness of God's love in my life, and it would flood over me in waves. Joy, joy, joy; so much sometimes that I could hardly handle it all. Gradually the joy flowed over even into the grief, and the frustrations, and the disappointments in my life. It wasn't that God always gave me the solutions to all my problems, but that, through the problems, God's presence was there: "the everlasting arms," "the Good Shepherd," "our rock and our foundation." I found myself trusting him, and loving him, more each day. I remember telling a friend, "I thought Christ would take away from my life, but instead he's added to it."

When the feminist movement began to establish itself, I viewed it as an attack on my Christian faith and reacted with a degree of arrogance and defiance. I had the vague idea that feminism and Christianity were incompatible. As I felt myself increasingly drawn into the women's movement, a struggle began in my life. If feminism and Christianity were incompatible, which would I choose? My Christian faith was not composed merely of a set of beliefs; it was an intensely close, personal relationship with Someone I loved very much. Yet the consensus among many Christians seemed to be that feminism was essentially "un-Christian."

As I considered it, I had to agree that, yes, some *feminists* were extreme in some of their beliefs, but that feminism, or the ideal of basic equality between women and men, was entirely consistent with my Christian faith.

Sorting out the complexities of my own beliefs and feelings amid my increased involvement in a very controversial movement kept me awake many nights. What I found particularly distressing was that much of the opposition to women's rights was springing up from among the people with whom I would expect to have the closest alliance: Christians.

I have since come to realize that there was a degree of naïveté to my faith that is common to young Christians. After coming into a personal experience with Christ, we find it inconceivable to think that others who have had the same experience could be anything but loving and supportive. I was bowled over by the hostility I encountered from a number of know-it-all Christians. During my frequent trips to the capital, or at public places where I was to speak, I found myself being challenged, interrogated, and, with less frequency, accosted, shoved, and threatened. The reasoning seemed to be that God was against the Equal Rights Amendment (and women's rights). And because I was for it, I was therefore the Enemy, and fair game.

In no time the Equal Rights battle became polarized and embittered. In all fairness, I'm sure that some proponents have done their share of behaving rudely. I found it particularly upsetting, however, that the opposition, coming from the religious sector, seemed to be characterized by such anger and hatred. And, yes, I found myself often responding with anger and hatred, and I didn't like it. I felt guilty about my anger and I tried (often unsuccessfully) to overcome it. Among opponents of the ERA, however, what comes across to me is their belief that their hatred is perfectly righteous and justified.

Of course not *all* Christians joined the antiequality

bandwagon; in fact, many of my richest Christian friendships developed from my ERA work. But it is a sad fact that throughout history there has been a tendency, within Christianity, to go to extremes; to take Christian liberty and turn it into license; to justify arrogance and self-righteousness against a cause which is deemed, often unjustly, as "un-Christian."

One reaction to this has been some real hostility toward the Christian faith among some feminists, as with my friend in Springfield. In another similar instance, I will never forget listening to a lecture by feminist author Marilyn French, author of *The Women's Room* (Summit Books, 1980). Her speech was earnest, compelling, and completely unself-conscious. As she spoke about the use and abuse of power, and about the vulnerability of women, I found myself moved to tears. After she spoke I was asked to say a few words, and I should have declined. I was so choked up that I fumbled all over the place like a blithering idiot.

Afterward several of us went to dinner. Marilyn French sat on the far end of the table from me (and got up only briefly to change the title on the rest-room door with a felt marker from "ladies" to "women," to our delight). After dinner I had a chance to speak with her briefly, and expressed how much her talk had meant to me.

"But," I said, "I don't agree with your denunciation

of the Bible. There are people who are reassessing these narrow interpretations . . ."

I was never able to finish. I felt like I had hit a raw nerve. She took off furiously, stating that, yes the Bible has some beautiful passages, but it is an awful book, a sexist book, a racist book, a war-mongering book. Her attack was not aimed at me, and I understood that, but it left me so surprised that I was able to respond with little more than "I disagree."

I have thought about that encounter many times since. Had I had the time, and the presence of mind, I could have argued round and round with her, but I doubt if it would have accomplished a thing. Her opinions were clearly immovable, as were mine. I thought later that trying to talk me out of my faith would be like trying to persuade me that the institution of marriage is an evil to avoid. All the reason in the world wouldn't mean a thing up against the fact that I love my husband and am very happily married. Period.

It's more than security, and it's even more than faith. It's love. God isn't someone I merely intellectualize about, or, for that matter, follow and obey blindly. God is someone, as I have stated before, whom I love.

It's in the framework of that love that I've been working my way through the changes in my life these past several years. My faith and beliefs are, obviously, decidedly Christian. At the same time, I am ashamed and angered by the creeping Christian chauvinism I see in much of the Christian right-wing movement today. It is entirely possible, I believe, to hold deeply felt convictions, while respecting, and even being open to learn, from the differing views of others.

But how does one strike a chord somewhere in the middle: between strong convictions and intolerance; between the Christians who claim God is an anti-feminist and the feminists who insist Christianity is anti-woman?

I have had a few moments when I wondered if I would be able to work my way through it all and still remain true to my convictions. But as the struggle progressed I knew . . . *I knew* . . . that I was both a Christian and a feminist, and that the two are complimentary, not contradictory. Working my way through the cobwebs and confusion became not a chore but an adventure; one that strengthened and confirmed my beliefs, all the way around.

4
THE CASE
FOR EQUALITY

It was a gathering of church women, and I had come to talk about the Equal Rights Amendment. Before I began, one older woman came up to me and said, somewhat defiantly, "I have worked all my life in the home, raising five children, and I'm proud of it. Now you're telling me that everything I've done all my life is worth nothing." When I began protesting that I was saying nothing of the kind, she countered, "But isn't that what this whole women's rights thing is all about?"

There is strong feeling about the importance of mothering in this society, and woe to anyone—especially the feminist movement—who appears to be challenging motherhood. Perhaps our slogans say it best: "motherhood and apple pie," "God couldn't be everywhere at once, so he created mothers," and "the hand that rocks the cradle rules the world." Although more women than ever today are working outside the home, many, if not most women who marry and have children expect to spend some part of their lives as full-time home-makers, or at least in only part-time outside employment. While the role of the homemaker may vary somewhat, the economic, social, and spiritual value of her contribution to society is immeasurable. When a woman gives up a career and puts aside an education to devote herself to the full-time care and nurturing of her family, she is performing perhaps the most important job in this country. Historically the woman as homemaker/nurturer has played a major role in the growth of this country. But the true gauge of the importance that society places on the homemaker's role is not in slogans, but in the position of that role under the law. It is there that we have been "weighed in the balances," to quote the prophet Daniel, and been "found wanting." The biggest shock of my life came when I began to discover the number of legal rights that women lose, depending on which state they live in, when they get married. It is perhaps the greatest betrayal of American womanhood that when a woman becomes a homemaker (which society encourages her to do), in doing so she may have actually *lost* legal rights and precious legal status that no other group in society is ever asked to relinquish.

Opponents of women's equality make much ado about the pedestal women are supposed to be on and insist that equality would be a step down.

While many women may feel that their families do put them on a pedestal, under the law the pedestal does not exist.

The U.S. Constitution and the laws in most states were written and adopted under the concepts of English common law, which was described in the eighteenth century by the English jurist William Blackstone as meaning that "by marriage, the husband and wife are one person in Law . . . the very being or legal existence of the woman is suspended during the marriage." The state of Georgia restated this doctrine in a 1974 law declaring that "the husband is the head of the family and the wife is subject to him; her legal existence is merged in the husband . . ." (Georgia Code, Ann., 53-501 [1974]).

Literally hundreds of laws are based on this principle. For example, in spite of the strong biblical charge to make sure that widows are provided for, in South Dakota a husband may disinherit his wife, except for her right to live in the family home for her lifetime. A Georgia husband may disinherit his wife; however, if she wants to, she may petition the courts for a year's support, to be paid out of her husband's estate. The "right" to live in one's own home, or to be supported for a year, are meager rewards indeed for a woman who may have devoted years of her life to her home and family.

In some states a wife may be denied the right to manage her own property, or she may be denied any say in establishing the family domicile. In Maine if a husband and wife jointly run a business, the profits from that business belong legally to the husband, not the wife, even if the wife is putting the most effort into running the business and the husband is not taking his share of the responsibility.

The laws vary from state to state, with some states being fairer than others. But the bottom line for women is that they are at the mercy of the courts and the lawmakers. This is because, while the U.S. Constitution clearly prohibits discrimination based on race, it was never intended to prohibit discrimination based on sex, and the Supreme Court has never interpreted it to do so in all areas. This is why changes have been patchwork at best, and very uneven.

Even when the laws do treat women fairly, the principle of common law is always under the surface, waiting to rear its ugly head. Its potency is perhaps best illustrated by the footnote found frequently in law journals which reads: "The above is not applicable to children, idiots, and married women."

In 1915, for example, the Supreme Court of Oklahoma ruled that "contracts between a husband and wife are invalid, because a wife has no legal existence" (Sodowski vs. Sodowski). Can you imagine a court ruling which says that black people, for instance, or Jewish people have no legal existence? It would be unthinkable! And yet today, in a country that takes pride in its concern for motherhood, we tell wives in many states that their legal status is precarious at best, and in some instances virtually nonexistent.

One dramatic illustration concerns a Wisconsin homemaker named Margaret Rasmussen. She and her husband, Harold, along with their two sons, lived in her mother's home. Harold brought home the paycheck and turned it over to Margaret, who did the family's bookkeeping, paid the bills, and rationed out money for household and personal expenses.

The Rasmussens didn't have much money, but Margaret believed that her sons should go to college, and she managed to save a little here and there for their education. Her mother also occasionally made a contribution to the college funds, and gradually the savings grew.

Margaret died in 1963, when her sons were teen-agers. She left her sons two savings accounts in their names, totaling $5,000. Harold remarried and moved out of his mother-in-law's house. That $5,000 seemed like a lot of money to him, so he went to court to get it. "I earned that money," he argued, "and I never gave it away. I merely entrusted it to Margaret to pay the bills. The surplus belongs to me."

What do you think the court said? Remember, there would have been no surplus without Margaret's careful economizing, not to mention her years of valuable, unpaid labor as a homemaker. Also, the family lived in *her* mother's home, and she had also contributed some to the education funds.

The court agreed with Harold, stating that ". . . the excess left after paying the joint expenses of . . . the family remains the property of the husband. . . ." The boys' college money went to Harold and his new wife. Margaret's long years of scrimping and saving to assure her sons an education were an exercise in futility. (The case is *Rasmussen vs. Oshkosh Savings and Loan Association*, 35 Wis. 2d 605 [1966]. It is referred to in *That Old American Dream and the Reality*, Wisconsin Governor's Commission on the Status of Women, Madison, WN, 1977.)

Margaret Rasmussen is just one of countless women who have fallen through the cracks of a legal system that fails to protect adequately the homemaker. Even the "right" of wives to be supported by their husbands, touted by some as being the mainstay of the American family, is actually entrenched in the common law principle which regards the husband as the head of the family and the wife as his property, and is for all practical purposes completely unenforceable in an ongoing marriage. A man can have lots of money, but spend it drinking and gambling; or he can be a miser and bank his money while keeping his family in poverty conditions. His wife can be the most devoted wife and mother in the world, but she has no legal means to obtain anything from him that he doesn't *choose* to give her, unless she breaks up her family, sues for divorce, and tries to obtain alimony. The so-called "wonderful right" of wives to be supported by their husbands, which is hailed by some as actually keeping families together, can in reality create reasons for splitting them apart! Although some married women do have a good life, it is only because a kind and generous husband wants it that way and earns enough money to make it a reality. It is certainly not because of the law!

These few examples make it clear that equality would be preferable to this kind of pedestal any day. Indeed, these laws are destructive to the family unit, immoral, and unjust. But more important, they are in *direct contradiction to the Word of God*.

Much of the rationale behind these laws has been the biblical injunction that the husband should be the head of the family and that wives should submit to their husbands. I do not believe that those few

Bible verses, taken out of context, are any justification for the kind of unfair laws which exist against wives and mothers. In fact, if the Scriptures are considered further, we find some very tough and specific requirements placed upon husbands, which define the kind of "headship" they are to have.

In the fifth chapter of Ephesians Paul says, "Husbands, love your wives as Christ loved the church." What a bombshell! There is no greater example of love than the love Christ had for his church. He went so far as to wash the feet of his disciples, and in one post-resurrection appearance even prepared dinner for them. Paul goes on in another passage to tell us that Christ "humbled himself and became obedient unto death, even death on a cross" (Phil. 2:8).

There we have it, the kind of Christlike love that husbands are to show their wives. It is not a love that lords itself over another, or arrogantly displays its authority. It is a *submissive* love; a love whose primary concern is for the other. The prophet Hosea offers an excellent example of this kind of love. While I certainly do not condone the adultery of his wife, Hosea's patience and faithfulness to her in spite of her unfaithfulness is a touching story, full of messages for today. The Bible tells us that Hosea's love for Gomer, in spite of her failings, symbolized God's love for Israel. It also illustrates the way Christ loves his Church, and the way husbands are to love their wives.

Given all this, can we continue to tolerate a legal system which regards women, and particularly married women, as second-class citizens? Would husbands who love their wives as Christ loves the Church expect laws to allow them to disinherit their wives, or to treat them unfairly in other ways?

Rather than reflect biblical principles, these laws literally deify husbands, and may even allow a husband absolute power over many areas of his wife's life.

While it is admittedly impossible to legislate Christlike love, it *is* possible to legislate fairness. We cannot force husbands to love their wives, but we can at least make sure that the law allows them no inordinate power.

Fortunately, most husbands are not inclined to take full advantage of these laws, and therefore most wives are spared the injustices. But that is no reason to bury one's head in the sand. The injustices are real, and to some women they are devastating. If our concern for motherhood is genuine, then the best thing we can do to protect it is to grant women full equality.

5
NIBBLED BY DUCKS

I was recently involved in a long-distance phone conversation, getting some information about the status of ERA in another state. It was 10:30 in the evening. One would certainly expect that at such an hour a phone call uninterrupted by kids would be possible. Not so. I was constantly being interrupted to say things like, "No, you may not eat a plum in bed; you'll leave the skins in the sheets," and, "Get in bed and don't poke your brother in the head again." And I found myself trying to solve such problems as "He keeps looking at me; make him stop," spoken in a shrill, desperate voice.

Finally, the children settled down and I said to my caller, "You know, sometimes I don't believe that I, a fully grown adult woman, actually have conversations like that."

A sympathetic mother of young children herself, she replied, "I understand. Sometimes I think having small children is like being nibbled to death by ducks."

Her comment brought about my biggest laugh of the day if not the entire week. I repeated it to several people the next day, and mothers invariably reacted as I did—with instant recognition and good humor. (The few men I consulted generally smiled and said something like, "What do you mean?")

Nurturing and caring for a family and raising children can be the most rewarding job in the world. It can also be the most thankless, the most frustrating, and the most boring job imaginable. And in the midst of this rewarding, frustrating job, the traditional homemaker is being pulled in different directions, dissected, and questioned about her role as never before. Small children aren't the only "ducks" that are nibbling her to death.

The women's movement of today has brought about a dichotomy and a polarization that some-times has the housewife right in the middle. When women's liberation came upon us in the late sixties, many of us didn't know how to react. It was the feminist movement that brought attention to the gross inequities between men's and women's wages (inequities that still exist, by the way, in spite of some dramatic gains). The movement also pointed out the rampant discrimination that made it difficult for women to get into such professions as law, medicine, journalism, and broadcasting. Most people heard about these inequalities and gradually

50

found themselves agreeing that, yes, this was unfair and should be changed.

But the women's movement seemed to be saying something else that made a lot of people uneasy. It seemed to say, essentially, that the woman who didn't work ouside the home was an exploited fool. I debated a woman once who declared that "those people" (women's rights advocates—presumably that included me) regularly refer to housewives as "drones" and "slobs." Needless to say, her statement made me very indignant. I have been working for women's rights for years and have never heard anyone use either of those terms. Nevertheless, in the early days the movement got stuck with the image of being antihousewife, and it has been a hard image to shake.

How did this idea ever get started? That question is not as simple as it may seem, and there are a lot of answers.

For one thing, the media reacted to the feminist movement as a big joke. Any action for women's rights in the late sixties was usually introduced in the news with a commentator saying, "Well, the girls are at it again," accompanied by raucous laughter from backstage. Dramatic events, such as the bra-burning episode (which actually never occurred) were played up in the news, and serious concerns were often ignored.

At the same time, I have to admit that the movement in those early days had an edge to it that was intolerant of the homemaker. The intolerance came in part from anger: anger at the hypocrisy of a society that encourages women to become home-makers, and a legal system that places them in a vulnerable and precarious position when they do. The only solution, some said, was radical sociological upheaval: denounce the traditional role of the homemaker and get all women employed outside the home.

I think to some extent this hard-line approach was necessary in order for feminism to establish itself as a valid, serious movement. It didn't take long for the women's movement to grow beyond this and, indeed, it is this same movement that has worked to improve the legal status and security of the homemaker by supporting programs that provide help for displaced homemakers and battered wives and fairer inheritance laws. But the early image of the man hating bra-burners remains, and has been cleverly exploited by a very vocal minority.

Predictably, the feminist movement has set off a reactionary movement, calling itself "pro-family." Included in this contingency are such strange bedfellows as ultrafundamentalists, Mormons, and right-wing Catholics. The rhetoric of this group is typical of any reactionary movement. By quoting the more extremist elements of women's liberation, it hopes to discredit the entire movement. It appeals to traditional women and says, in effect, "They're out to get you! You have a wonderful, privileged position, but if you don't watch out, they'll take it all away from you!" There are heavy undertones of a conspiracy and a lot of scary propaganda, such as, "We all have the wonderful right to be supported by our husbands" (implying that the minute husbands are no longer afraid of going to jail they will immediately abandon us), or "They want to take us down from our superior position, take away our wonderful rights, and make us equal."

The problem with this is that it is a gigantic lie. An extreme example illustrating the uncertain status of married women (which was outlined in the previous chapter) involves a woman named Selina Martin.

Selina lived in Louisiana, a community property state, which said until recently in its laws that the husband is "head and master" with "total control" over all community property. Yearly attempts to change this law in the legislature were unsuccessful, and even one compromise proposal, recommending that the control be 75 percent for the husband and 25 percent for the wife also failed.

In 1978 Selina was working double shifts as a nurse to support her unemployed husband and pay the mortgage on their home. Her husband decided that he wanted to take out a second mortgage on their home. To Selina's dismay she could not prevent him from doing so, even though their home was jointly owned, and *even* though she was the breadwinner for the family. Louisiana law described the husband as "head and master" and gave him the right to do as he chose with their jointly owned property, unhindered. Then, to her added dismay, she found that she was *totally liable* to pay for the second mortgage that she could not prevent him from taking!

Selina Martin went all the way to the Supreme Court of Louisiana protesting this law, and in May of 1978 she *lost* her case (Selina Martin vs. Corpus Christi Credit Union), as well as the home that she had worked so hard to acquire for her family. That same year, the United States Supreme Court *refused* to hear the case.*

The good news to this story is that the Martin case brought public attention to the injustice of the Louisiana law, and shortly thereafter the legislature

*Thanks to Kim Gandy, an attorney at law in New Orleans and former assistant district attorney of New Orleans Parish for helping me put this information together.

finally voted to change the law, giving the husband and wife equal control over community property. The cost to bring about this change, however, was Selina Martin's home—a mighty heavy price to pay for justice.

It should be noted here that the new law did not go into effect until January 1, 1980. In 1979, before the revision went into effect, legislation was introduced to repeal a large portion of the newly passed revisions, the effect of which would have been to leave the head and master provisions intact. That bill was defeated in committee by *one vote*. The fact is, American women are completely dependent upon the kindness and good graces of courts and legislatures for their rights—courts and legislatures that change every year. That will remain the case until the Equal Rights Amendment is added to the constitution.

It has been observed that many women tend to overestimate their legal rights. It is just this false sense of security that gives the "pro-family" movement its base of support.

"Pro-family?" What an ironic title! It boggles the mind to believe that denying women sure legal recognition as persons and denying full partnership in marriage can in any way strengthen the family! The notion is nothing new. When women wanted the right to an education, to enter the professions, or to vote, the argument always lifted up was that it would destroy the family. The lack of logic in such a philosophy is obvious. As Walter Lippmann observed, "We do almost no single, sensible, and deliberate thing to make family life a success. And still the family survives. It has survived all manner of stupidity. It will survive the application of intelligence" (*Drift and Mastery*, Peter Smith).

I have come to believe that "pro-family" is nothing more than a positive term which is used to describe what is essentially a very negative movement. Groups that prefer to identify themselves this way have, in fact, a very small opinion of the family. They believe that it cannot survive unless wives are robbed of freedom, denied job and education opportunities, and perhaps even the right to vote. (This is not as ludicrous as one might think. The state of Mississippi has, as of this writing, steadfastly refused to ratify the Nineteenth Amendment, granting women the right to vote. We may be thankful that at least that right is guaranteed to women in the Constitution.) "Pro-family" would make wives utterly vulnerable and at the mercy of their husbands. This is denied, of course, and a lot of rhetoric is heard about protecting women's "superior rights." I believe, however, that the true feelings of the so-called "pro-family" movement are summed up in the statement of Howard Phillips,

National Director of the Conservative Caucus, speaking at a "Pro-family Rally" on July 12, 1980, in Long Beach, California—a rally sponsored by the California arm of the national group called "Moral Majority" (the California group calls itself "Citizens for Biblical Morality"):

A second major result of policies that have been anti-family, that have begun not just in this decade or even in this century, but have extended for many years, have been the liberation of the wife from the leadership of the husband. It has been a conscious policy of government to liberate the wife from the leadership of the husband and thus break up the family unit as a unit of government.

First, in the 1800s legislation was enacted which freed the wife of economic dependence on the husband, or at least that trend was initiated as women were given—women who were married and members of families—were given property rights which previously women exercised only when they were widows or unmarried, or family heads in their own right.

Second, we saw how women were liberated from the leadership of their husbands politically. You know it used to be that in recognition of the family as the basic unit of society, we had one family, one vote. And we have seen the trend instead toward one person, one vote.

It is no wonder that the modern American housewife, observing all this, feels that she is between a rock and a hard place. On the one hand is the women's movement, which many have interpreted as looking down on traditional values and the homemaker. On the other hand is the reactionary, anti-feminist movement, claiming to protect rights for her that for the most part do not exist, and claiming that anyone supportive of women's rights is not a real woman and has obviously rejected her chosen role. (A word they use a lot is *frustrated*.)

I don't believe that the answer is in either extreme. The feminist movement was right in pointing out that the legal status of the homemaker is not wonderful, and that something is terribly unjust about a society that uses her unpaid labor while robbing her of legal rights. It is not unladylike, or for that matter un-Christian, to speak out against injustices. The Bible is full of stories about men and women doing just that. And I think it is terribly unfair to dump responsibility for the low status of homemakers on the women's movement. After all, it wasn't the women's movement that coined the phrase "just a housewife."

But the solution is not to get rid of the title "homemaker" and abolish the traditional role. What is wrong is the law, and the deeper, underlying societal disregard for the value of that role, which the law reflects.

Recognition of the homemaker's nonmonetary contribution to the family welfare as being of equal value to that of the wage earner should be written into the family laws of every state in this country. For example, because of the equal rights provision in Montana's 1975 State Constitution, new legislation explicitly recognizes the economic worth of the homemaker and reads: "Insofar as each is able, the husband and wife shall support each other out of their property and labor . . . the word 'support' includes the nonmonetary support provided by a spouse as homemaker."

More important, however, and more complex, it should be written into the hearts of every one of us. When we use the terms "working woman" or "working mother," aren't we implying that the woman who raises a family, runs a home, and participates in countless volunteer programs isn't doing *real* work? Homemakers are frequently left off advisory boards unless they have some other title. The title "homemaker," by itself, is rarely enough. I am never introduced as simply a homemaker, and I find that women who are involved in other activities rarely include the title "homemaker" in their descriptions of themselves.

The homemaker's job is often the least appreciated

of anyone's. Other jobs include status reports, promotions, raises, and bonuses. But the faithful housewife is easy to take for granted. My mother once asked me why I took the time to make homemade noodles for my family, and I replied, "Because they never thank me when I clean the bathroom."

Perhaps the greatest indication of the low value that is placed on the homemaker's work is the difficulty middle-aged women, who have never worked outside the home, have finding employment. It is a terrible thing that unless a woman has done salaried work she is presumed to have no experience of any value to an employer.

And finally, as if to add insult to injury, countless television commercials, from "ring around the collar" to the "Snoopy Sniffer" and the "Ty-D-Bol Man" are based on the presumption that the American housewife is the world's biggest ninny. (Can anyone imagine a commercial where the guilty party being told about "ring around the collar" is a *man*?) I have long contended that the success of Phil Donahue's daytime talk show has been due, at least in part, to his inclination to treat the American housewife as a being with some degree of intelligence.

So, the opponents of women's rights are wrong to say that everything was just hunky-dory for the housewife until the women's movement came along. But it is equally wrong to forsake the housewife, blaming her for the ills that society has put upon her. She is a very important person, doing a very important job.

Every homemaker has felt, on occasion, that she is being "nibbled to death." But if the people around her genuinely appreciate and value her, and if the laws recognize her as a partner and an equal contributor, then perhaps all those other little "ducks" will be easier to bear.

6

"I'M NOT
A WOMEN'S LIBBER,
BUT ..."

In mid-1978 I was asked to be a guest on a nationally syndicated television talk show. After a brief introduction I began to field a few questions, when the host suddenly asked me, "Are you a feminist?"

I didn't flinch; I smiled. And I answered evasively, "By some definitions," and then quickly changed the subject.

No one, friend or foe, ever challenged me about that statement. I doubt if anyone even took note of it. But it left me feeling guilty and uneasy, for what reason I wasn't quite sure.

I had what I thought was a good defense for my evasiveness. I have heard the word *feminist* used by some opponents of the Equal Rights Amendment, and what *they* mean when they label someone with that title is *not* what I am.

I am not a man-hater. I don't hate children. And I'm not out to force women into full-time careers, or destroy families. (I have, however, received countless letters and anonymous phone calls accusing me of being guilty of all of this and more. It's best to develop a sense of humor quickly when working for a controversial social issue!)

I reasoned to myself that labels can be so misleading, and that in promoting the Equal Rights Amendment I didn't need that excess baggage. Who needs all the images that appear in some people's minds with the word *feminist?*

But I still felt guilty. For some reason, being evasive didn't seem quite honest, particularly in this instance. Besides, I have never cared much for fence-sitters. Refusing to align myself with a movement that has done so much for women seemed the height of cowardice.

Years earlier, before I became active in the ERA battle, I had used a similar cop out. I believed in equal pay, equal credit rights, and equal property rights for women. I supported help for rape victims and battered wives. In principle, I saw the reasonableness behind many of the causes that were being championed by the women's movement. And so, when the subject of "women's lib" came up, I made what I thought was a very bright, original, and generous statement. (It was, I've since learned, neither bright nor original; and it wasn't very generous, either.) "I'm not a woman's libber, but . . . ," I would say, and then go on to add progressively, "I believe in equal pay for equal work . . . ," and so forth. It was a neat way of agreeing with the goals that the women's movement was fighting so hard to attain, while separating myself from the movement.

It didn't work very long. I began to realize that major corporations did not wake up one morning and say, "My goodness, we're paying our female employees half what we're paying our male employees. We must straighten that out!" Nor did banks, as a whole, suddenly begin to give women equal credit rights out of the goodness of their hearts. And legislatures rarely began to straighten out unjust rape laws all on their own. These changes were coming about because the women's movement was fighting so hard to bring them about. Before long the hypocrisy of the "I'm not a women's libber, but . . ." syndrome began to dawn on me.

One time a leader of a so-called "pro-family" group smugly said to me, "*We* support the Equal Credit Opportunities Act" (assuring women of equal credit rights). It wasn't until after our conversation that it dawned on me that the Credit Act had already passed and become law several years earlier. How convenient, I thought angrily, to support something *after* it is passed. The true test, of course, of what one really supports and believes in is in what one does *before* it comes about. And who was supporting and fighting for passage of the Equal Credit Opportunities Act beforehand? Who else? Not the anti-feminists; it was the women's movement.

But if rejecting the women's movement while supporting its goals is hypocrisy, then why do so many people seem to be doing it? I mentioned that the "I'm not a woman's libber, but . . ." excuse is not original; in fact, I hear it all the time. A number of women want all the things that the women's movement has fought so hard to achieve for them, but don't want to be identified with the movement.

Why is this? I think part of the reason is that the early image of the bra-burning woman's libber remains. The women's movement has grown and matured far beyond its early rigid militance. Too often, however, public understanding of it has not. Many people still believe that it takes a certain type of woman to be a feminist.

"I object to the term *feminist* because those women are the most *un*feminine women alive," one woman told me.

A friend recently asked me why I seldom buy pant suits and instead always wear skirts. I told her that when I'm traveling and speaking for ERA I feel I must wear a skirt. Some people are so sure I can't be a real lady, that I take every precaution to prove that I am.

I do it, but I have to admit it's ridiculous. It's an old refrain. When the early suffragists were fighting a similar battle to obtain the right to vote, one jeer that became familiar to them was, "What do you want to be? A man?" Whenever women want first-class citizenship and recognition as full and equal human beings, they are accused of being unfeminine and of wanting to be men.

There is a difference between being *equal* and being the *same*. Feminists don't want to be men. In fact, as a whole they are a group of women who have enormous pride in their womanhood. They enjoy being women, and they have great respect for other women.

But they do want equal opportunities with men, and they do want equal justice under the law. They want to be recognized as having equal value as men, and they don't want to be prejudged by society merely because of their sex.

Beyond that, the feminist movement is as diverse, complex, and even contradictory as any group of people can be. Feminists are not uniformly agreed on all issues. They have different political views, differing moral values, and different religious beliefs. The notion that a feminist must be a certain type of woman (i.e., militant, unfeminine, nontraditional, nonreligious, unmarried, against or ambivalent toward motherhood, and so forth) is absurd.

And while I'm on the subject, I feel I must object to the very disgusting and offensive term "woman's libber" (with its variations, "women's lib," the "libs," and the "libbers"). Many people who use this term aren't aware of how insulting it has become. It was coined by the press in the late sixties when the women's movement was not considered to be a very serious movement. While the press has grown up in its attitude toward the women's movement, opponents of women's rights have not. Just as the suffragists were jeeringly called the "suffs," modern-day proponents of women's rights have been labeled by their opponents as "women's libbers." It is nothing more than a cheap shot; a nasty, derisive label intending to belittle and discredit supporters of women's rights.

While I remain uncomfortable about labels, and the way they can so easily be distorted, the bottom line for me is that I want my daughter to grow up in a world that treats her equally and fairly, and where opportunities are offered to her on the basis of her capabilities as an individual. And that is what the feminist movement wants, and is working for.

A few months after the TV show, I was asked by a newspaper reporter whether or not I considered myself to be a feminist. This time I didn't hesitate. My answer was positive and direct, "I sure am!"

7

THE GOSPEL ACCORDING TO THE FAR RIGHT

A few years ago I was asked to address a group about my activities on behalf of women's rights, and the way it all related to my Christian faith. I began by saying, "There are a number of ultraconservatives in this country who believe that a true Christian is one who opposes the Equal Rights Amendment, the Panama Canal Treaty, and the fifty-five mile an hour speed limit."

I meant it as a joke but, as I was beginning to discover, that flip statement contains a great deal of truth . . . and it isn't so funny.

Since I began getting publicity in my role as an equal rights advocate, I have been called a lesbian, a prostitute, a communist, and a false prophet, always by Bible-believing, Scripture-quoting Christians. I have a friend who relates being chased around the lawn of the state capital in Springfield, Illinois, by a lady(?) wielding a sign which read: "Stop ERA," and screaming, "You're going to burn in hell!" I witnessed a minister, no less, dressed in a monkey suit, prancing around the lawn of the

68

Illinois capital, handing out bananas bearing the message, "Don't monkey with the Constitution!" All the while a group of his supporters were singing in the background, "God Bless America."

These examples may be somewhat extreme, but increasingly, religious leaders are taking conservative to ultraconservative stands on various political issues, claiming to speak for God and representing all "true" Christians. Their answers to the problems of the world are often self-righteous and simplistic. Their rhetoric is characterized by a paranoia that seems to say, "All who disagree are a part of the enemy and are plotting together against us." Another effective tool is guilt-by-association: choosing the most controversial supporters of the opposing view, with the implication that these people really represent *all* who share the view.

The far right is not new to American politics. It has long been characterized by fear, emotion, and vindictiveness. In a world of increasing uncertainties and changing, confusing values, however, its simplistic message is especially seductive.

I am aware that all of this sounds a little strong. But the seriousness of this right-wing Christian movement was brought home to me recently in the case of Patricia and Stanley Gundry.

For eleven years Stan Gundry was a professor at Moody Bible Institute in Chicago. His wife,

Patricia, was a homemaker, and in 1977 she wrote a book *Woman, Be Free* (published by Zondervan), a nonradical, thoroughly scriptural appeal for equality of women and men in the church.

There were no shock waves when Pat Gundry's book was published. It was well received by a number of evangelical Christians, and was considered a valuable contribution to the ongoing debate about the biblical view of women. After its publication, Pat was a guest speaker on Moody Bible Institute's radio station, and as late as November 1978, was invited to participate at a women's symposium held at Moody.

Then, in March of 1979, Pat Gundry was the guest speaker at a local Housewives for ERA* meeting in Glen Ellyn, Illinois. Five months later, her husband was fired from his position at Moody Bible Institute with no warning, under circumstances that are less than clear.

The Housewives for ERA meeting began innocently enough. Pat began her talk by reading the story in Genesis which declares that both man and woman are created in the image of God. She then

*Housewives for ERA has since changed its name to Homemakers' Equal Rights Association. Terri Wedoff is the national president, and I am president emerita. For more information about HERA, see the last pages of this book.

asked the question, "Who was the first feminist?" The answer? God, of course. She proceeded to give her very logical appeal for equality of men and women from a biblical, theological point of view. Her talk was nonpolitical. "I didn't go there to speak on the Equal Rights Amendment, or any other political issue," she said. "There are other people who can do that. I know about biblical feminism, and that's what I talk about. I feel that it is very important for people to know that God doesn't hold women to be inferior people."

Attending the meeting were a handful of stop-ERA women. When they were given the opportunity to speak, it became quite apparent that they weren't there to gain from or contribute to the meeting in a positive way. They were, as one of the Housewives for ERA members later observed, "out to get Pat Gundry."

"They asked hostile questions, trying to get me to say something they could write Moody about," remembered Pat. "It was the typical scare thing, with lots of guilt-by-association. They kept bringing up unrelated issues, controversial things, to get something they could use against me."

(It is to her credit, several people told me afterward, that Pat remained poised and gracious throughout the meeting, and never once evidenced the angry, self-righteous tone of her inquisitors.)

Shortly after the meeting, the letters to Moody Bible Institute began. Before long the campaign against the Gundrys began to snowball. Pat Gundry was rejecting the Bible, they said. The Reverend Wayne Van Gelderen, pastor of the Marquette Manor Baptist Church in Downers Grove, Illinois, urged in a radio program for listeners to write to Moody Bible Institute. His appeal was emotional. "I was shocked," he said ". . . if you love the gospel, love Moody Bible Institute . . . write a letter."

He told his listening audience, "It's not a time for anger. It's a time for grief. It's a time, as you're shocked about it, to realize we're losing institution after institution. This is how you lose them. Just a little bit here and a little bit there, with blatant, liberal tendencies, and we've lost them all."

He concluded: "Oh, friend, would you help me today? Would you help on this? I think you can do more good than anybody if you will write a letter, and if you will do it right now."

Other ultraconservative churches joined the letter-writing campaign, and before long Moody was getting mail from around the country, objecting to Professor Stanley Gundry and his infamous wife, Pat.

In all of this, Pat was being thoroughly misquoted. For example, when asked at the Housewives for ERA meeting about her feelings on the drafting of women, she replied, "I find it no less abhorrent to send my son to slaughter than my daughter." Letters to Moody quoted her as saying, "I would be just as willing to send my daughter to slaughter as my son." The word-twisting is slight but clever, deliberately distorting the thrust of her remarks.

Her attackers claimed that her book denied the Scriptures; that it was socialist and Marxist. When pressed, however, most admitted that they had never even read *Woman, Be Free*. In fact, it is a soft-sell, very moderate treatise, based entirely and with great care on the Bible. While one might disagree with her conclusions, to deny her commitment to scriptural authority is absurd.

Privately, many of these people admitted to her that this was nothing personal. "It has nothing to do with you, or you husband, or even your book," she was told. "It's really because you have endorsed ERA."

It's estimated that Moody received about seventy letters. (Exact figures are unavailable, since Moody has been so closed-mouth about the whole Gundry affair.) All of this apparently began to make them nervous, because in June they informed Professor Gundry that he was not to discuss the feminist issue in the classroom, since his views were in conflict with the institute.

In his years as professor, Gundry had been

known for his fairness and objectivity. When social issues were discussed he encouraged consideration of all views. He would often, at the conclusion of a class share his own opinions, but always in a tolerant and open-minded way. There had never been any complaints about his feminist views which, while he didn't flaunt them or impose them on others, were no secret. *Why did Moody Bible Institute suddenly find them so objectionable, after eleven years?*

In addition, at that time Moody had *no* official position on feminism! While the Institute did not allow women to enroll in the pastoral major, in its evening school it both accepted and trained women who were ordained and functioning as pastors. "By no stretch of the imagination does MBI have a clearly stated position on this matter," Stan Gundry observed at the time of his dismissal. "At best it is ambiguous; at worst it is self-contradictory." It should be noted that since the Gundry episode Moody *has* adopted an official position on women, but at the time of Stan's firing they had none, as he stated.

Nevertheless, on August 1 Professor Gundry was asked to resign from his position at Moody Bible Institute. (At one point an official at MBI even threatened a legal suit against the Gundrys to recover revenues lost by the Institute, allegedly due to their activities.)

The public relations office of the Institute issued the following statement: "The position of Dr. Gundry and his wife regarding the feminist movement and, therefore, the role of women in the church is objectionable to the administration and trustees of the Moody Bible Institute, and is the basis of his resignation. A fair and honorable separation was agreed upon. Because this is a personal matter, we have no further comment." Moody Bible Institute has refused to make any further statements about the case.

In a memo to an official at Moody before his forced resignation Gundry observed: "These letters contain half-truths, misrepresentations, and outright lies. You also know that this campaign against Pat and me was initiated and helped along by a far-right wing element that thrives on innuendo and controversy." One Housewives for ERA member who attended the Glen Ellyn meeting that started the whole thing put it a bit more bluntly. "This is nothing but McCarthyism," she told me, "that same syndrome. It's absolutely disgusting."

Pat and Stan Gundry insist that he was not fired from his job because of his (or her) theological views about women. In an interview with the Chicago *Sun Times* (September 20, 1979), Pat asserts: "It's a political situation caused by stop-ERA activists conducting a smear campaign based on slander, innuendo, and distortion directed at Moody Bible Institute in order to get them to take a political stand against ERA. The explanation is money and power."

It does appear that Moody caved in to a great deal of pressure from people who admitted that their concern was more political than theological. Among right-wing Christians, the distinction between the two is not always so clear.

The religious right is, predictably, against women's rights, abortion, gun control, arms control, homosexual rights, help for displaced homemakers or battered wives, government aid for child care centers (or, for that matter, *any* child care centers), the International Year of the Child . . . to name only a few. I find myself agreeing with their positions on some issues, but I believe that the real concern is not the validity of their positions on the various issues. That is secondary. What concerns me is the mind set of the right-wing Christian; the attitude which says, "I-speak-for-God-and-if-you-don't-agree-with-me-on-this-you-are-against-God." What often follows is the belief that "that-gives-me-the-authority-to-attack-you-and-discredit-you-in-any-way-I-see-fit!"

Watching the right-wing Christian movement grow over the past several years, I have come to several conclusions:

It appeals to emotion rather than reason.

Nowhere is this more apparent than in the knee-jerk anti-feminism of the religious right. The picture is painted of a bunch of evil, man-hating, tough women, who are plotting to destroy families and tear mothers away from their babies so that they can be put to work in cruel factories. Never mind the many vocal activists for women's rights who are happily married, have been homemakers, and are far removed from this description. (First ladies Betty Ford and Rosalynn Carter, and homemaker/columnist Erma Bombeck come to mind as examples.)

In July of 1978 I marched with my husband and our oldest son in a national rally for the Equal Rights Amendment in Washington, D.C. It was the largest women's rights march in history. We were with a Housewives for ERA delegation which included wives, mothers, and several families. The same day we heard a leading opponent of the amendment on national television call the marchers "radicals and lesbians." The fact is that as many as ninety thousand people marched in Washington that day, representing such diverse groups as churches, unions, and Girl Scout troups. But *radicals* and *lesbians* are hot-button words designed to stir emotion. Reason was sacrificed for an appeal to hatred, prejudice, and fear.

It judges Christians by their political rather than their religious beliefs.

When Pat Gundry left the Housewives for ERA meeting, where her simple discussion caused such an uproar, one of the stop-ERA women turned to her and said, "I fear for you on the Judgment Day," apparently because of her alignment with a pro-ERA group. (Ever the lady, Pat replied confidently, "I'm not afraid.")

I have been told countless times that I cannot possibly be a true Christian. The reason? Because of my support for the Equal Rights Amendment. I always reply that I have not yet found the Bible verse which says, "Oppose the Equal Rights Amendment and thou shalt be saved."

Actually, what the Bible says is: "Believe on the Lord Jesus Christ, and thou shalt be saved" (Acts 16:31 KJV). So, the basis of my Christian life is my faith in Jesus Christ; *not* my political views on *any* issue. Yet the religious right has been characterized by an often vengeful intolerance which defines the depths of one's faith by one's political views.

Intolerance, of course, has no political preference. Liberals can be just as bitter and narrow as conservatives. But the religious right makes this intolerance on political issues particularly unbearable, because it claims to speak for God. (If God is against the Equal Rights Amendment, for example, then in supporting it I am going against God.)

I submit that Christians are going to have diverse political views, but they must be secure enough in their faith at least to accept and respect one another, even if they do not always understand.

It is an end-justifies-the-means philosophy.

I am intrigued by my children and their childish view of the world as they watch reruns of the old "Batman" and "Lone Ranger" TV shows. In their young minds life is very neatly divided in two kinds of people: the "Good Guys" and the "Bad Guys." There are no shades of gray. In this world, the Good Guys are always, uncompromisingly on the side of right.

It is this simplistic, black-and-white view of the world which, I believe, most characterizes the gospel according to the far right. Given this mind-set of perfection and self-deification, an end-justifies-the-means attitude is inevitable. Being one of the Good Guys, on the side of absolute and unerring truth in all matters, gives one license to make personal attacks against anyone on the other side, to twist the truth, and to employ the tactic of guilt by association. It justifies a judgmental, intolerant attitude.

In a child this mind-set is understandable and amusing. In an adult it can be frightening and even

dangerous. It is exactly this kind of thinking, carried
to its extreme, which led to the Crusades of the
Middle Ages, to countless religious wars and, most
recently, to the capture and bondage of fifty-three
American hostages in Iran.

*It is negative and seeks only to preserve the status
quo.*

In 1977 I participated in a regional "International
Women's Year" meeting held near the campus of
the University of Illinois in Urbana. Several
anti-ERA women came to the preliminary work
session, and were encouraged to participate in the
planning of the event. They said very little, except
to voice opposition to making free day child care
available, because of a desire to "avoid all forms of
socialism." They left their names and addresses but
follow-up letters sent to them were returned
marked "addressee unknown."

Controversial issues such as the Equal Rights
Amendment and abortion were eliminated from the
program, because it was felt that discussing these
issues would serve no purpose other than to
polarize the participants. The planners wanted
instead to find issues that would be of concern to
women on both sides of the feminist issue. The idea
was to bring both sides together and find some
mutual concerns.

Opponents were scarce and uninterested when given the opportunity to do some of the work and planning for the event, but the day of the meeting they came in large numbers. A lawyer was the main speaker; her topic was the varying legal rights of women. Her talk was deliberately unsensational, but the anti-ERA women and men had come for a confrontation, and a confrontation they had. In the middle of the lawyer's speech, they stood up and demanded the podium. Several of them finally marched up to the platform and grabbed the microphone away from the speaker and began raving about the evils of IWY. It was chaos.

Later that day I was a participant in a workshop on the legal rights of homemakers. On the panel with me was a lawyer who had taken no public position on the Equal Rights Amendment and a Mormon woman who was against it. That did not satisfy the opponents. Several came to the workshop with a collective chip on their shoulders because I was a vocal ERA advocate. Each panelist gave a short presentation, and we opened the floor to questions. Sure enough, several persons in the audience began questioning me in a manner indicating that they felt it was their divine mission to challenge me on ERA. One woman came to the podium, Bible in hand, and, first singling me out, preached an emotional sermon, saying that we were all surely going to hell if we didn't turn around on ERA.

One man quizzed me relentlessly about the amendment. His tone was hostile; he obviously wanted to draw me into an open fight on ERA. I had been asked to avoid such a confrontation, and I did, so he accused me of being evasive. When the day was over, I was later told, he left a briefcase behind. Not knowing whose it was a custodian opened it. Right on top was a paper with the heading: "How to Disrupt a Meeting."

This was a huge shock to me. Until that time I had never fully recognized the negative nature of the anti-feminist movement. I really believed that we could plan a positive, constructive meeting with these people. But the religious right does not operate in a positive way. It stands *for* the maintaining of the status quo *against* any changes. Again and again women have told me that they are *against* the Equal Rights Amendment, or *against* shelters for battered wives, or *against* help for displaced homemakers, or this or that program to benefit women, because "any woman who would get herself in that predicament deserves what she gets," or because "*I* don't need to be liberated." What it so often comes down to is: "I don't care about anyone else. As long as I'm happy, I am against any change, any disruption of the status quo." Often clouded in high-sounding emotional words about God, morality, and the family, the gospel according to the far right is, in fact, a *negative* gospel; as such it is in conflict with scriptural principles.

Jesus told Peter, "Upon this rock I will build my church; and the gates of hell shall not prevail against it" (Matt. 16:18 KJV). For years I believed that that meant Christ's church would stand as a rock of morality, undaunted as the forces of evil moved forward to try to tear it down. But the word *prevail,* in fact, indicates the reverse: that the *church* will be a moving force for good in this world, going forward so that the forces of evil will not be able to stand or prevail. The church is not standing still, protecting the status quo. It is a force moving against hatred and prejudice; against despair and poverty and fear. The gospel of Jesus Christ is not a negative gospel; it is a *positive* gospel; a gospel of compassion and caring, a gospel of the love of God.

I have, in the past, described a liberated woman as one who has experienced the redemptive grace and forgiveness of Jesus Christ and who knows that she is a whole and a valuable person in the eyes of God. I am a Christian, and for me, at least, that has been my liberation. But it is a cop out to leave it at that. It would be the height of hypocrisy for me to tell women who write to me asking my help because they cannot find fair employment and are unable to support their children, or have been disinherited or raped or beaten by their husbands, "Don't worry, Jesus loves you," and end it there. There are social imperatives to the Christian gospel as well. If I am to be a force for good, then it is not enough to talk about my faith; I must also live it.

The example of Jesus speaks more emphatically to this problem than anything else I can say. The sinful, immoral, despised people of his day were the ones for whom he cared the most. He identified with them, reached out to them, and made his place among them.

And who did he find the most contemptible? Not the immoral pagans, but the smug, self-righteous religious people.

Well, today there is a smug, self-righteous trend in the Christian faith that is characterized by a lack of concern for anyone outside the status quo and, which is worse, divine justification is given to this uncaring attitude.

The last thing I am suggesting is that the solution is a counter-Christian movement taking perhaps more liberal stands on some of these political issues. But we do need to be wary of anyone who seems to be more concerned about the political than the religious views of a fellow Christian. The result can be a bitter divisiveness which can be crippling to the Body of Christ.

I recently asked an anti-ERA leader who organized religious people against the amendment if she thought anyone could be a Christian and support the Equal Rights Amendment. She hesitated and then said rather nervously that, no, she didn't see how that could be possible.

Slam. With those words any possibility of our finding some middle ground of belief and concern was closed to us. She was a woman I liked, too. She had a friendly personality, a great sense of humor, and an abundant faith. I would like to have gotten to know her better. I was sure we had some common interests and beliefs. We certainly shared the same faith in Jesus Christ.

But in her mind no common bond of faith could make up for our political differences. She identified and labeled me as one of "them" before we could explore any possible basis for friendship.

What a waste.

8
CINDERELLA
AND OTHER FICTION

Is there such a thing as a proper formula for a perfect marriage? With the much publicized "breakdown of the family" these days, there are a great many people coming forward, claiming that a perfect-marriage formula does exist, and more, that they know exactly what it is.

I can't be too critical, however. There was a time when I thought I knew everything about how to make a marriage work, too. That was, of course, before I got married.

Shortly after I was married I happened to hear an animated speaker talking about her husband. "People are always asking me if I have ever considered divorcing him," she began, assuming a facial expression of mock indignation. "I have *never* thought of such a thing," she continued. "Murdering him, yes, but *never* divorcing him."

This silly line struck me as being so hilarious that I practically fell out of my chair laughing. I had spent most of my life waiting for my prince to come. I completely believed the Cinderella story that once I found "Mr. Right" all my problems would be solved, and I would live happily ever after, completely fulfilled to be someone's wife.

A few months into our marriage and the awful truth was dawning on me: "Mr. Right" expected me to entertain his friends on a moment's notice and to iron his permanent press shirts; he had a lousy disposition in the morning, and if something made him angry, he could give me the silent treatment for days. I began to believe that Cinderella was nothing but fiction, and that happily-ever-after was someone's idea of a joke.

My husband had, of course, more than his share of postmarriage revelations, as well. And I found it all more than a little disconcerting. I had been sure that if we agreed on major issues (religion and politics), and if we loved each other, the rest would be easy. All the love in the world aside, it was not always so easy. And rarely was the source of contention any major issue. It was the little things: like the morning he woke up and couldn't find a matching pair of socks in his drawer, or the afternoon when I waited an hour in near blizzard conditions for him to pick me up from the bus stop.

I look back on this today with amusement. When I got married, I was so sure that I had all the answers. Often, though, when the problems came along, none of the answers fit. I was walking into a complex adult relationship with the simplemindedness of a child.

I think of this today when I hear the simple answers that are coming forth from many sectors in the Christian community regarding marriage. Isolated scripture passages are quoted to set up a divine plan for marriage: the husband is the head, the wife is subject to him and must submit to his will. (The marriage theology often goes to the extreme of the divine "chain of command" theory, in which husband submits to Christ, wife submits to husband, children submit to wife. Many advocates of this system believe that a wife may not go directly to Christ, only through her husband.)

There are variations. Some go so far as to say that the wife must not manage the family finances, that the husband is to be the primary provider, and that the wife should not work outside the home. Some relegate the wife to the position of complete powerlessness, encouraging manipulation if she is to have any input in the relationship. Others allow for differences, but insist that when there is a deadlock, God ordains that the husband's will prevail. Always.

Book after book is written in which the proper formula for the "right" kind of marriage is laid out. Aside from being tedious, I believe that much of this simplistic theology is based more on cultural values than scriptural truths. For example, there is no biblical basis for requiring women to stay home.

In fact, Bible women pursued various careers: the virtuous woman described in Proverbs 31 was, among other things, a shrewd businesswoman; Priscilla in the New Testament was a tentmaker with her husband, Aquila (see Acts 18).

In addition, I find the excessive preoccupation with the headship of the husband and the obligation of the wife to submit lopsided and distorted. I believe it reflects the prejudices of our time more than it does the biblical ideal. It sets up a double standard, which places the primary responsibility for a successful marriage on the wife.

She is told not only how to be properly submissive, but also how to be "total," "fascinating," "the wife of a happy husband" (so now she's fully responsible for his happiness!), adoring, and fulfilled. The message is that no matter what problems exist in a marriage, if a wife will only get her act together, everything will be fine.

The implication that the Bible places greater responsibility for proper behavior on the wife is utterly groundless. In fact, if we are to take the Bible quite literally, it could well be argued that the greater responsibility lies with the husband! Several passages remind husbands to be gentle, loving, sensitive to a wife's needs, and Christlike in the marriage (see Eph. 5:25-33; Col. 3:19).

I am, however, inclined to suspect simplistic

answers of any persuasion. I do not believe that the balance of power can, or should be, weighed and measured so precisely—"the husband's job is this, the wife's job is that"; "the husband should behave this way, the wife should behave that way." Rigid, legalistic formulas are inadequate, and often unfair and confining, in dealing with the complexities of adult relationships.

The message of the entire Bible, and particularly of the New Testament when viewed as a whole, is the love and grace of God manifested in Jesus Christ. The basis for Christian relationships, then, is not the law, it is love; it is not a rigid formula, or a balance of power; it is Jesus Christ.

I am encouraged that a number of biblical feminists are coming forward and dealing with the apparent contradictions, the paradoxes, and the difficult passages in an effort to shed new light on the biblical view of marriage. I will leave to them the complex Bible exegesis. The main theme that seems to be emerging, however, as the narrow, legalistic views are challenged and the biblical message as a whole is being considered, is *mutual* submission.

"Submit yourselves to one another," Paul told the early church at Ephesus. Then, further down, he gets specific: "Wives, submit yourselves to your husbands." "Husbands, love your wives just as Christ loved the church" (Eph. 5:21, 22, 25 TEV).

How anyone can eke out of that a system in which the husband always has the final say and has total control I will never understand. It is a gross distortion of Scripture to quote the one verse ("Wives, submit yourselves to your husbands"), and lift that out of context as though it is the summary of Paul's remarks. When the entire passage is considered, it is quite obvious that the summary verse is the first one, which encourages people to submit to one another in all their relationships.

In this passage, while wives are told to submit, husbands are given the example of Christ. And, if we are to define submission as humility and selflessness, then Christ was the most submissive person who ever lived! He gave up "equality with God" and chose to take on human form, submitting himself to death on the cross (Phil. 2:6-8). He washed the feet of his disciples, and in one post-resurrection appearance even prepared a meal for them (John 13:3-17; 21:7-13).

I once heard a minister preach that wives were to submit themselves to their husbands as unto the Lord, "even when their husbands were not very Lordlike." The other side of the coin, which he characteristically neglected to mention, is that husbands should also love their wives as submissively and selflessly as Christ loved the church, even when their wives are not very lovable.

91

The biblical view of marriage, and of all relationships, is radical indeed. Using the example of Christ, the ideal marriage is one in which both partners throw away the scorecard and give without being preoccupied about whether or not the other one is keeping up his or her end of the arrangement. Minute divisions of whose job is what and who should behave exactly what way serve to erect barriers to grace and love and to hinder the working and leading of the Holy Spirit in people's lives.

At this point someone always says, "Yes, but . . . when a husband and wife reach a point at which they cannot agree, it is the husband's job to make the final decision."

Here we go again. Another legalistic, inflexible rule. When my husband and I can't agree about what car to buy, we try to work out a compromise. If we get deadlocked trying to find a compromise, he makes the final decision—about the car.

If, however, the subject is new dining room furniture, *I* make the final decision. Does that mean that we are not following the Bible correctly?

But those are minor disagreements. What about when the husband gets a terrific job offer in another town, but his wife doesn't want to move? An uneven interpretation of the Bible is likely to lead to the admonition that it is the wife's job to submit, and therefore, like it or not, she must go (many laws are based on this principle; see chapter 2).

But in a balanced interpretation of the Bible, then the husband's obligation to be loving and sensitive to his wife's needs must also be given attention. She may have a job of her own which she enjoys and is unwilling to give up. She may have friends and family and roots where she lives that she will be unable to replace anywhere else. She may be shy and fearful of change. If a husband loves his wife in the way that Christ loves the church, then he will not just pick up and move without consideration for his wife's side of the dilemma.

But then, what's the solution? When we set the husband up as a demigod with the final say in all things, and when we dismiss all the wife's feelings as selfish if she happens to feel differently, then the solution to all disagreements is simple: we do it *his* way. There is a part in each of us that would like things to be simple, clear-cut, and uncomplicated. Mutual submission, with genuine Christlike concern for each other, can be terribly complicated.

In the case of the husband who wants to move and the wife who doesn't, there is no pat answer. Ideally, the couple will discuss it and pray about it, consider each other's feelings and needs, weigh the pros and cons of each side, and make their decision to go or stay based on their own particular situation.

It's a lot harder than the mandate to do things the husband's way, period. But it is, I believe, the best way.

Moreover, it disturbs me that the simple answers of some marriage theologians all but ignore cases in which the ideal appears unattainable. For instance, they are adamant about no divorce. But what about cases when a partner is repeatedly unfaithful, or when one is abusive, either physically, verbally, or emotionally? Since the emphasis in so much of this ideology is on the wife and her obligation to submit-and-take-it-no-matter-what, I have found that in these cases, it is the wife of an unkind husband who is apt to suffer the most. Many women who are married to decidedly un-Christlike husbands who may be cruel, excessively self-centered, or just plain childish and irresponsible face a sort of double jeopardy: not only must they endure it; they often are made to feel guilt for their husband's behavior. Constant emphasis from religious leaders on the wife's responsibility to submit, never to excel in a way that might threaten her husband's ego, or never to presume to give him advice or express her disapproval of his behavior often serves only to dump unnecessary and unfair guilt on a woman trapped in what may be a horrible situation.

Mutual submission means that marital obligations are mutual; but I don't believe it means that either partner must forever submit-and-take-it-no-matter-what. Just where to draw the line when one partner is trying and the other is not I don't know. These situations are difficult, and often tragic. I find divorce abhorrent and believe that every effort should be made to make a marriage work. But, any discussion of how to behave toward one's mate must also include the acknowledgment that one's behavior may not be reciprocated. Christ himself could not always stir a response from everyone for whom he showed love and concern. Christians must begin to accept and minister to the unfortunate exceptions to the ideal of two partners loving each other in a mutually submissive manner.

In I Corinthians 13, the famous love chapter, Paul sets forth the ultimate ideal for all relationships: the agape love which finds its example and its source in Jesus Christ. He describes love as follows:

> Love is patient and kind; love is not jealous or boastful; it is not arrogant or rude. Love does not insist on its own way; it is not irritable or resentful; it does not rejoice at wrong, but rejoices in the right. Love bears all things, believes all things, hopes all things, endures all things. Love never ends . . . when the perfect comes, the imperfect will pass away. (I Cor. 13:4-9)

"When I was a child," Paul concludes, "I thought like a child . . . when I became [an adult], I gave up childish ways." Paul recognized that the child in all of us yearns for a simple, legalistic formula, inflexible and pat, so that we never have to struggle through uncertainties as to what our roles should be. But the true biblical ideal for marriage is something far more complex and risky and exciting: a mature relationship based on mutual submission, understanding, and love.

9

THE MATRIARCHS

A few years ago I attended a Bible study in which I, rather timidly at first, dared to challenge the leader on his narrow view of women. The discussion deteriorated quickly in a back-and-forth Scripture quoting contest. He dredged up the verses telling women to be silent and to exert no authority over men. When I suggested that, taken in context, those passages were obviously intended for the immediate situation but not for ever-and-all-time, he protested that I was twisting the Scripture to suit my purpose, and what would happen if everyone did that? I asked if *he* might be twisting the Scripture to suit *his* purposes, and round and round we went.

Finally I said to him, "What about Deborah?" There was silence. Then he said, "You mean the prophetess?"

For all his knowledge of the Bible, he wasn't even sure who Deborah was! Deborah was a great deal more than a prophet, as I was only too glad to tell him. In fact, Deborah alone countered all his arguments about women. If God wanted women to assume such limited roles, I asked, why did he raise up Deborah?

During the period of the judges, Deborah emerged as the only woman judge of Israel. A woman judge? A woman determining right action for others, without a man helping her make weighty decisions? Yes, and more.

Her courtroom was a palm tree, and people came from far and wide to sit under Deborah's palm tree, air their disagreements, and have her settle their disputes. As told in the fourth and fifth chapters of the Book of Judges, Deborah was highly regarded and known for her perception and wisdom. She must have been a remarkable woman to rise to such a position of honor and respect, especially in a day when women were normally dominated by men.

The Bible describes her as being not only a judge but also a prophet: one called to proclaim and set forth the Word of God. She lived during a time when Israel was being oppressed by the land of Canaan, whose military captain was a man named Sisera. It was Deborah's leadership that resulted in a breaking of the bonds of oppression.

She sent for a man named Barak and ordered him to lead an army against Sisera's army. "The Lord God of Israel commanded . . . I will deliver him into thine hand" she prophesied. (See Judges 4:6-7.)

98

Barak agreed to go, but only if Deborah would go with him. He apparently needed her leadership and judgment.

Deborah did go with him, and as she had foretold, Sisera's army was beaten back and utterly destroyed.

When I first read the story of Deborah, I felt as though I had found hidden treasure. I had read the Bible for years. I knew all about David and Samson and Saul and Abraham, and umpteen other men. I found their stories exciting and inspiring, but why had I never heard of *Deborah* before?

Several years ago I attended a study on women in the Bible, and it made an impression on me that I will never forget. The group was first divided in two sections, each with a large chalkboard and some chalk. The first group was asked to write on the board all the named men in the Bible that they could think of. I was in the second group, and our job was to write on the board all the women in the Bible that we could think of. Both groups were given the same amount of time.

Needless to say, the list of the first group was three times the length of ours. I thought, well, there really aren't that many women in the Bible who did anything, anyway. We were then handed a list of the named women in the Bible, including their main accomplishments. The list was ten pages long! I was astounded. I had read, studied, and loved the Bible for many years, but I had never heard of half of these women. The stories centering on the men I knew well, but somehow most of the women had been lost to me.

The point of all this was, of course, to illustrate the church's neglect in giving attention to biblical women. Since then I have devoured the stories of Bible women and relate them with enthusiasm at the slightest provocation.

The women of the Bible speak for themselves. They defy all stereotypes, even modern-day ones, to which we might try to confine women. They didn't wear any labels, but in a patriarchal society, they emerge as matriarchs, and their stories have instilled within me and countless other women a great pride in the faith of our mothers.

Take Sarah, for instance, who is remembered as the wife of Abraham. Closer consideration, however, proves that she was more than that: she was the mother of a great nation.

Genesis 16 tells the story of God's promise to Abraham. For years that's all I thought it was: a promise to Abraham that his descendants would become a great nation, through whom all the nations of the world would be blessed. I have heard the terms "seed of Abraham" and "son of Abraham" used to describe people of faith. (Christians believe that Abraham's nation, the Jewish people, brought Christ to the world; therefore, those believing in Christ are "of Abraham.") Not until I sat down and really looked at the Scripture did I realize that God gave the promise to Sarah as well! In Genesis 17:16 he says, "I will bless her, and she shall be a mother of nations." At one point Abraham's concubine bore a son for him, but God decreed that the heir to the promise would not come through just any woman. In the same way that God chose Abraham, he had *chosen* Sarah.

No big deal? It is when you consider the time in which it is written. The culture of the day regarded the wife as property, put in the same category as cattle and land. For God to declare that the blessing was to come forth from Sarah as well as from Abraham was amazing, even revolutionary. Shortly after studying the life of Sarah, I led a small group of women in a worship service. We concluded by affirming ourselves as the "daughters of Sarah." That designation is wholly scriptural and valid, but it had been years before it ever dawned on me to refer to myself, and other women of faith, in such terms. When I finally did I felt a flood of joy and sisterhood that I cannot describe. I did not realize, until that moment, how excluded I had felt from so much of traditional worship.

Other women who shine in my heart include

Rahab, the harlot from Jericho who saw the greatness of the God of Israel and aided his armies when they came into her land (Josh. 2). She is mentioned twice in the New Testament as an example of great faith (Heb. 11:31; James 2:25), and she is listed in the genealogy of Jesus (Matt. 1:5).

When Jesus said, "Blessed are the peacemakers" (Matt. 5:9), I like to think that he was thinking of Abigail (I Sam. 25). When her husband Nabal, who is described as "churlish and evil in his doings" (KJV), refused to provide food and clothing for David's army, David became so angry that he vowed to kill Nabal and everyone in his household.

But when Abigail, described as "a woman of good understanding, and of a beautiful countenance," heard of her husband's rudeness, she immediately packed food and drinks, rushed to David, fell on the ground, and begged forgiveness for her husband's stupidity. David was grateful that Abigail's intervention prevented him from acting impulsively and violently; so grateful that when Nabal died, David married her.

Abigail's actions showed immense courage, wisdom, and diplomacy. Imagine confronting an approaching army that has just been insulted by your husband! She prevented untold bloodshed. The world could use a few more peacemakers like Abigail!

And then there were others: Anna, the prophetess who worked in the Temple and was one of the first persons to acclaim Jesus as the Messiah (Luke 2:36-38). Esther, the Jewess who was queen of Persia and who acted bravely to save her people from a plot to exterminate them; Joanna, wife of Chuza who left her home to follow Jesus during his earthly ministry (Luke 8:3); Phoebe, a deaconess and minister in the early church (Rom. 16:1-2).

These are just a few illustrations of the many women in the Bible; women who did not always fit the norm. We need to look at them, study them, get to know them, and identify with them. No, they weren't perfect, but considering the patriarchal society in which they lived, many of them lived amazingly liberated lives.

These women have much to offer us, and exist alongside the men in the Bible as great role models for our children and examples for ourselves. I am convinced that encouraging greater recognition of them will serve to strengthen the fellowship within the church. It will lead to heightened appreciation for the contributions that women can make among the men and to a greater sense of worth and purpose among the women. It will also open up countless illustrations for sermons and discussion groups that have previously been overlooked.

I ought to know. I'm a daughter of Sarah!

10

THE MOTHER LOVE
OF GOD

Once when I was a little girl, I was in a Sunday school class where the members were asked to describe God. I remember the enthusiasm as we all tried to top one another with our descriptions.

God has kind eyes. God has a long, flowing white robe. God makes thunder when he walks. God has a strong, booming voice, but he can whisper if he wants to. God is love, God is holy, God is powerful, God knows everything.

And, of course, God is a man. We pictured him with a long white beard, resting on a giant cane. To our little minds, God was the ultimate father figure.

To many of us, the image of God as a man remains fixed and immovable. Some feminists today have reacted to this view by asserting that God is perhaps a woman. In each case, God is being anthropomorphized—spoken of in human terms. This is not necessarily blasphemous or inaccurate; many times in the Bible God is anthropomorphized. For example, when Isaiah said of God that the earth is his footstool (66:1), he was anthropomorphizing God. The description brings to mind a person so huge that he may sit back and rest his feet on this planet. Of course this passage is not meant to be taken literally; it means only to describe the enormity, power, and greatness of God so that we may keep our own visions of greatness in perspective.

The Bible refers to God in masculine terms ("him," "he," "father"), but it also uses a great deal of feminine imagery to describe God. In all this, God is being anthropomorphized—brought down to human terms and spoken of in a way that we might understand. In reality, however, God is neither a man nor a woman, and I believe we minimize God when we try to confine him absolutely to our human categories.

I was one who grew up thinking of God as a man, and that is a hard image to shake. I would have thought anyone peculiar who might have challenged that view. God is "father," "king," and "Lord"; not "mother," "queen," or "lady"! But as I began to study some of the descriptions of God in the Bible, I found some surprises.

One of the most striking is contained in the trilogy of parables in Luke 15. Two of them are rather familiar to most people: the story of the prodigal son, who takes his inheritance early and leaves home, only to return later where he finds, to his surprise, that his father warmly welcomes him back; and the story of the shepherd who leaves ninety-nine of his sheep to go find the one that has gone astray. In each of these stories the message is clear: God loves and cares for each of us in a special way, the way the father loved his son and the way the shepherd cared for his sheep. In each we see a symbol of God in both the shepherd and the father.

But this is, as I said, a trilogy: there are *three* stories here. The lesser known of the three is about a woman who lost a valuable coin and proceeded to sweep her house and turn it upside down until she found it. When she did she called her neighbors together and invited them to come rejoice with her that the lost had been found. In the same way, the message is that God rejoices when people find their way back into his love and care.

What is all but ignored in the telling of this story is the fact that, like the waiting father and the good shepherd, the woman who loses and then finds the coin *also* represents God. Jesus was using the image of a woman to symbolize God! It would seem, just from this one example, that our narrow perception of God as a man is rather shallow.

This is a subject that must be approached with extreme caution. It is easy to be misunderstood, and many people become easily inflamed at any hint that the deity may contain female characteristics. In talking about the characteristics of God in an adult Sunday school class once, I brought up some of the feminine imagery for God that is found in the Bible, and was met with a stony silence. Finally, one woman blurted out that the whole subject was stupid, and what difference did it make, anyway? She told me later that she may never get her husband in church again since I had said God was a woman. (I never said that!) She pointed out that the ancient pagan religions, with their fertility rites, worshiped goddesses, and wasn't I suggesting that we revert back to such paganism?

There was no explaining it to her but, no, that is not what I was suggesting. In fact, I believe that the rigid view of God as a man is more similar to a shallow paganism than the understanding that *man* or *woman* are just human terms that may be used to describe a God who, in reality, transcends all our feeble efforts of description.

Her question, "What difference does it make?" hit a chord with me. It forced me to wrestle with myself over the question of whether or not this issue is worth the trouble and confusion that it invariably raises. I decided that it was.

It was not a radical, liberal feminist who put it in terms that touched me most deeply, but Pope John Paul I, the "smiling pope" whose short reign of one month was characterized by his warmth, humility, and compassion. In one of his regular Sunday Angelus blessings in St. Peter's Square he said: "He is Father. Even more, God is Mother, who does not want to harm us" (*Time*, September 25, 1978, p. 88).

As a mother, I am very sensitive to just what mother love is. A number of Scripture passages allude to the mother love of God. Two in particular hold great meaning for me.

In one God says to Israel, "Can a woman forget her sucking child . . . ? yea, they may forget, yet will I not forget. . . . I have graven thee upon the palms of my hands" (Isa. 49:15-16 KJV).

I have carried two babies for nine months, watched the miracle of their entrance into the world, and held them to my breast and nurtured and loved them in their first hours. My third child was just a few weeks old when we adopted her, but when I first looked down at her tiny little form in that cradle I saw her as *my* baby. I swept her up into my arms and felt all the flood of mother love that I experienced when first looking at her brothers.

I remember the feeling of vulnerability that came over me when my first child was born. I had never before had so much to *lose*. This little person was such a gift; such a trust. I knew that I would die before I would let harm come to him.

It would be an insult to suggest that men cannot

have these same feelings, for I know they can. But in a society where the emphasis on nurturing is placed on the woman, it is the mother's love that we best understand. And it is this mother's love, we are told, that God feels for us. In fact, God says, his love for us is even greater. He finds the greatest human bond that we can understand, the love of a mother for her child, and says that his love exceeds even that.

In another passage, Jesus looks out over the people of Israel and says: "O Jerusalem, Jerusalem, . . . How often would I have gathered your children together as a hen gathers her brood under her wings, and you would not" (Matt. 23:37). Here again is the illustration of nurturing, protective mother love, showing us how much Christ cared for the people of Israel. "I want to protect you from sin and temptation; but you refuse my protection, and it breaks my heart." What mother cannot identify with that kind of love?

What difference does it make? It matters because when we are secure enough in our faith to see the whole of God (or as much of God as we might understand), God is not viewed merely as a stern authority figure, but as one whose concern for us is compared to mother love. And we learn that, by whatever terms we describe him (masculine pronouns, feminine imagery), God is really much greater than any of our descriptions, or any words we might use.

There is more to it than this. I am a woman. If God is a man then I am an inferior creation. But the Bible tells us that both men and women are created in God's image (Gen. 1:27). That statement means a great deal to me. If women are created in God's image just as men are, then our narrow perception of a masculine God is incomplete.

We have traditionally divided up human traits into masculine and feminine columns. Men are logical, analytical, and objective; women are intuitive, emotional, and subjective. But few people fit perfectly into either category. And just as people are a "mix" of these traits, and not predictable because of gender, so God is a "mix" of the authoritarian, analytical, *masculine* image, and the compassionate, intuitive *feminine* image. The mother love of God and the father love of God are really one and the same. Perhaps the masculine terms are used because we would not readily accept the authority of a woman, and the feminine imagery is used because most of us understand the love of a mother for her children.

God is, of course, the father waiting for his son, the shepherd seeking out his sheep, "King" and "Lord," and all the other masculine imagery with which we are so familiar. But something quite beautiful happens to us when we see that God is also the One who brings us forth in birth; who suckles and nurtures us; who wants to protect us under a wing of love. This wonderful imagery, which has been so neglected in our understanding of God, affirms the tenderest moments in our lives; it affirms our acts of service and compassion. It also affirms the value of women, and of men, who are joint heirs to the kingdom of heaven, created equally in the image and likeness of a great, great God.

JESUS'
SPECIAL MINISTRY
TO WOMEN

Alan Alda's definition of
the term *feminist* is my favorite. He says that a
feminist is someone who believes that women are
people.

It really is just that simple. There are so many
subtle ways in which women are treated as being
not-quite-persons—legally, socially, and emotionally: from dominating husbands to patronizing
doctors, to legal and economic inequities, to the
insults of pornography. The feminist in me is the
instinct that sees how these messages demean and
dehumanize women and that says, "I will not be
relegated to brainless servant, or fawning patient,
or cheap labor, or ornament, or object. I am a
person!"

Nowhere is that conviction more affirmed in my
life than by the person of Jesus Christ.

When I first picked up a copy of Leonard
Swidler's much talked about article "Jesus Was a
Feminist" (in the *New York Times*, December 18,
1971, p. 29), I was a little offended. After all, I

thought, Jesus isn't a *feminist* . . . he's the Son of God! But as I read on I was warmed by Mr. Swidler's description of a Christ who, again and again, in the midst of an oppressive, male-dominated society, affirmed the value and the wholeness and the worth of women. And I have found myself thinking, "I knew this all the time! This is what drew me to Jesus in the first place!"

I have a hard time putting my finger on what it is about the modern, cultural Jesus that makes me uneasy, but I think I finally have it: in a effort to make Jesus palatable to modern tastes, we have been turning him into one of the boys.

I am annoyed, slightly offended, and bored to tears with what I've heard called the "Christian Jock Syndrome": the almost cultlike hero-worship of the big, he-man Christian athletes. The message seems to be: "Jesus was no sissy and don't worry, you don't have to be either!"

Am I the only one who has observed that the various Christian athletic groups that have sprung up all over the country are *all male*? Of course they are! The "jock syndrome," combined with its macho image of Jesus, would hardly be effective with women.

This trend is not limited to the athletic sector but is found in all areas of life as well. It's so easy to allow our values to be determined by the world we live in, with its emphasis on materialism, immediate gratification, success, and prestige. Christians are just as prey to this as anyone else, with, of course, the added twist of justifying our values as a Christian virtue; molding Christ to fit our image rather than ourselves to fit his.

Of course Jesus was strong, dynamic, authoritative, and uncompromising. But he was no macho "man's man." He reached out to the sick, the poor, and the most despised around him and, for whatever sociological or cultural reasons, the "most despised" were very often women.

When I come to Jesus, I come to him as a woman. And as I read the New Testament, one thing becomes clear to me: Jesus had a very special ministry to women. He treated them unlike anyone had ever treated them; he often valued them more than they valued themselves. Dorothy L. Sayers observed in *Unpopular Opinions* (Victor Gollancz Ltd., 1946, and *Are Women Human?* (InterVarsity Press, 1971):

Perhaps it is no wonder that the women were first at the Cradle and last at the Cross. They had never known a man like this Man—there never has been such another. A prophet and teacher who never nagged at them, never flattered or coaxed or patronised; who never made arch jokes about them, never treated them either as "The women, God help us!" or "The ladies, God bless them!"; who rebuked without querulousness and praised without condescension; who took their questions and arguments seriously; who never mapped out their sphere for them, never urged them to be feminine or jeered at them for being female; who had no axe to grind and no uneasy male dignity to defend; who took them as he found them and was completely unself-conscious. There is no act, no sermon, no parable in the whole Gospel that borrows its pungency from female perversity; nobody could possibly guess from the words and deeds of Jesus that there was anything "funny" about woman's nature.

This remarkable attitude of Jesus toward women is evidenced throughout the Gospels. One of my favorite examples is the story of the woman at the well in John 4. She was a Samaritan, and Samaritans were looked down upon by the Jews. She had the reputation of a harlot. And, of course, she was a woman.

But Jesus went right up to her and began to talk to her. The Scriptures tell us that his disciples came back and were surprised to find him talking to a woman (treating her as if she were a person!).

Interestingly enough, he was there for more than just casual conversation. Jesus treated her not only as a human being, but also as a person of intelligence for whom he had respect. He told her about "living water," and she was one of the few people to whom he revealed his true identity. In a world that did not regard women as people, it was to a woman that he revealed these great spiritual truths. To him she was not a sex object or an object of scorn or contempt. He valued her as a whole human being. His disciples didn't understand, but I imagine that she did.

Everyone knows the story of Mary and Martha (Luke 10:38-42). Martha worked dutifully in the kitchen while her sister, Mary, boldly sat at the feet of Jesus to learn from him. Sitting at the feet of a great teacher was a privilege that was reserved for the men, and Martha was dismayed at Mary's audacity.

I think there is a bit of Martha in all of us. She was so preoccupied with the busy-work that had to be done, with fitting properly into her "role," that she couldn't stop to consider the deeper things in life. I suspect that Martha was also a little threatened by Mary. She felt a certain pride and security in her household role, and here was Mary, behaving most unwomanly. Perhaps Martha felt jealous and unappreciated. She believed that the biggest contribution she could make was in preparing the meals and in cleaning up afterward. But Christ was encouraging Mary to do something that women were not supposed to do: to sit and learn; to ask questions and to use her mind! Christ loved Martha, and he respected her work, but he knew and respected the mental and spiritual qualities of women as well. And so he told Martha that Mary had chosen the better part, and it would not be taken from her.

Luke, the physician, tells the story of a woman who had had "an issue of blood" for several years (Luke 8:40-48). Much like someone who had had leprosy, she was a woman who was considered unclean. She was not allowed to participate in worship, or in any social event. She was an outcast no doubt despised by many. Imagine what that had done to her sense of self-worth! She timidly touched the hem of Christ's robe, hoping to slink away, unseen. But Jesus turned and confronted her. He saw past her illness, past all the prejudices of his time. She reached out to him meekly; he turned to her and called her "daughter," and declared publicly that she was healed.

In a similar story, an unnamed woman (believed by tradition to be Mary Magdalene) washed Jesus' feet with her tears in the home of Simon, the Pharisee (Luke 7:36-40).

Simon was offended by the scene; he wanted to know why Jesus was allowing this sinful woman to touch him. I get the impression that Jesus was saying to Simon in his reply, "You could never understand." He told the story of two people, one who owed a small debt, and one who owed a great debt. When both of their debts were canceled, he asked, who was the most grateful? The one who owed the greatest amount, of course.

Of course. And the woman, whose sins were many, was able to appreciate the forgiveness, the wholeness, and the love that Jesus offered far more than could a respectable, "righteous," religious person like Simon.

And, of course, Simon didn't understand. One who has always felt valued and important is not likely to appreciate love and acceptance as much as one who has felt despised and unwanted. And this, I believe, is at the heart of Jesus' special ministry to women.

In an adult Sunday school class recently we were discussing Christ's death, when one person observed, "At his darkest hour all of Jesus' closest friends deserted him."

After a brief pause I spoke up. "No they didn't," I said. "The women didn't desert him."

To Dorothy Sayers' observation that women were first at the cradle and last at the cross I would add: and first at the resurrection. They were the ones who stood by as he died, and then went to the tomb to anoint his body. It was a world in which a woman's word was held to be so worthless that it was not valid even in a court of law. And yet it was to a woman that Christ first revealed the greatest event in history: the resurrection.

Why this special devotion for Jesus that is evidenced by women time and again throughout the Gospels? Because when others thought women to be unclean, Jesus saw through to their faith and declared them pure and spotless; when others thought women to be good only for physical labor, Jesus saw them as three-dimensional thinking beings; when others saw women as flighty and irresponsible, Jesus saw them worthy of bearing great truths.

Even today, when women are not always valued as being full and whole human beings, what may be the most unusual, appealing thing about Jesus is that he sees them as being just that.

He spoke with authority and claimed equality with God; he thundered through the temple; he healed the sick, raised the dead, and forgave sins. But what I find the most amazing is that, in his eyes, regardless of the values with which the world may judge women, he sees them as valued, important, worthwhile individuals.

119

12

OUT OF THE COCOON!

Several years ago, when I was just beginning to get into all of this, I found myself alternating between uncontrollable excitement and adventure, and uncontrollable panic and fear. During one of my brighter moments I was happily relating some of my new-found discoveries to my husband at about a mile a minute, barely stopping to catch a breath. My hands were waving excitedly and my descriptions were (to say the least) verbose. He finally told me impatiently, "Slow down! Slow down! For heaven's sake, you get so carried away!"

"That's easy for you to say," I retorted. "You're not the one who always thought you were a caterpillar and just discovered you're a butterfly!"

Of course in coming out of the cocoon I had been in, I was taking a terrible risk. As dark and limited as it was, my old way of looking at life and at myself contained a measure of warmth and security I wasn't sure I'd find on the outside. I admit, there have been times I've wished I had never taken that

first step, but as I look back on it, the good has far
outweighed the bad.

The women's movement that was such a jolt a
decade ago has opened more doors for me than I
could ever have imagined. When I took my first
faltering steps into my state capital to lobby for
women's rights, I didn't even know who my
legislators were. When I took on my first job as ERA
Coordinator in my district, I didn't know how to
write a simple press release. But I surely know
those things now!

I feared that my new outlook would cost me my
marriage, but I found that working together in a
partnership of mutual concern is a far greater
foundation for a marriage than trying to live
according to the childish pattern of fixed and rigid
roles.

I feared that it would cost me my traditional
values. All my life I have wanted to be a homemaker
and mother, and I was so afraid that feminism was a
threat to these beliefs. Instead the beliefs I once
held because of cultural influences are based on
intense conviction. Everyone says they care about
the homemaker, but talk is cheap. (I'm reminded of
the bumper sticker which reads, "If you love Jesus,
TITHE. Anyone can honk!") I have recognized the
inequities that are dealt the homemaker under the
law, and the lack of real respect that the homemaker

receives from all areas of society, and have been moved to fight for greater recognition of her contribution. In doing so I have come to believe in the value of the traditional roles of women more than ever. It is a masculine (and I might add secular) value system which says that earning money and making it in the business world is what is important. As a feminist, I value the nurturing and the caring that women have traditionally done as infinitely worthwhile. It becomes particularly meaningful when it's something that women choose as equals rather than have imposed upon them as inferiors.

I feared that the movement would cost me my self-worth. I perceived feminism as being a denial of woman's true nature and therefore a form of self-hatred. Even as I began to get involved I was afraid that I might turn into an aggressive, contemptible man-hater.

Well, I've been at it a long time now. Aggressive? Sure, sometimes. Contemptible? Well, I suppose there'll always be people who'll see it that way. Man-hater? Never!

But what about my own self-esteem? It has never been better. I'm sure part of that is due to the experience of working for something I believe in, something which will benefit other people and ultimately our society as well. Working with the diverse, wonderful women all over the country who are so committed to women's rights hasn't hurt, either. For a long time we jokingly called ourselves the "Old Girl's Network," because we work together as a support system and as sources for information. But lately some have been calling our connections the "New Woman's Network." I love it!

More is involved, though, in my improved self-esteem than that. It is absolutely invigorating, I confess, to be freed from the notion that my worth is attached to someone else: as so-and-so's mother and so-and-so's wife. No way! I love being a mother and wife, but that's not where my identity lies. My identity lies with me, in what I do. I am, first and foremost, not someone's wife or daughter or mother; I am me. And I find I like being me just fine!

Most immeasurably, though, my faith and my love for Jesus Christ have grown. The very special ministry that Christ had for women has touched me more than anything through my growth in the past years. In a world where women have never been regarded (in spite of all the rhetoric to the contrary) as being of equal value to men, Jesus Christ values them as full and whole human beings. I don't think I'll ever get over it!

Of course, I continue to work my way through a lot of tough questions. We have no pat, simplistic

formulas to see us through the changing roles of
women, and we should be leery of anyone who
claims to have it all too neatly figured out. There are
extremist voices on both sides of the issue, and
finding a path somewhere in between is no easy
task.

There are times when I don't feel so terrific about
being me; when the marriage partnership is a pain,
if not impossible; when being a homemaker appears
to be more laundry and dirty dishes than nurturing
and fulfillment. (Would you believe me if I told you
otherwise?) But overall, my increased involvement
in and commitment to the women's movement has
been an adventurous, positive, growing experience; one which, in varying degrees, has touched
the lives of countless other women like myself.

I'm reminded of an experience I had several
years ago at a gathering of women who were
married to ministers. I went, rather self-conscious
of my emerging feminism, which I was sure would
render me completely out of place. On the
contrary! The discussions ranged from the discrimination women face in the job market to breaking out
of the mold of the "minister's wife." I found, to my
amazement, that the growing awareness that was
going on in my life was happening to them, too!

I have come to believe that if you scratch any
woman in the right place, you'll find the makings of

a feminist. She may deny the label ("I'm not a woman's libber but . . ."), but the instinctive response to society's narrow view of women is there. As the role of women continues to change, the feminist in a lot of women is getting closer and closer to the surface.

Thinking back to that group of women, many of us were homemakers. We shared a common faith, had traditional values, and, for the most part, each enjoyed life in the parsonage.

But, like so many other women, the women's movement has made its mark on us; and we will never be the same again.

HISTORY OF THE HOMEMAKERS'
EQUAL RIGHTS ASSOCIATION (HERA)

HERA began as Housewives for ERA, an *ad hoc* group of Illinois women who came together to counter the image that housewives were against ERA. The main organizer then was JoAnn Budde, a woman in Evanston, Illinois. I joined right away, but made no organizational efforts.

In 1975 I started a local chapter of HERA in Champaign, and JoAnn asked if I wanted to take over the state as well. I agreed to help her organize a statewide meeting, and as we walked into the meeting (which was attended by only a handful of women) she said to me, "I'm going to nominate you as president." It was there that we elected officers for the first time (I was the first elected president), established bylaws, and dues. (Until that time Housewives for ERA had operated mainly as an extension of the Illinois ERA effort.)

In 1978 we held our first national convention in Springfield, and became then a national organization. In 1979, in a convention in Wichita (with Judy Carter) we became the Homemakers' Equal Rights Association. The name change reflects our concern to go beyond the Equal Rights Amendment, and to work for the betterment of the homemaker's legal and social status in all areas. (We still believe that the best way to do that, of course, is to ratify the Equal Rights Amendment.) Our initials HERA also happen to be the name of the Greek goddess of home and hearth, a symbolism that we believe is appropriate. We now have active chapters in twenty states, and we continue to grow.

Article I
Name and Symbol

The name of this organization shall be The Homemakers' Equal Rights Association, hereinafter to be abbreviated to HERA. The symbol of the organization shall be the pink rose.

Article II
Beliefs of HERA

Section A. We believe that the homemaker makes a valuable contribution to our society.

Section B. We believe that the institution of the family is vital to our society, and that the nurturing and care of the homemaker is important to keeping the family unit healthy.

Section C. We believe that the principle underlying the law in many states which regards the wife as the property of her husband places the homemaker in an unfair, precarious position under the law, and is destructive to the family unit.

Section D. We believe that laws should recognize the homemaker's non-monetary contribution to the family welfare as being of equal value to that of the wage earner, and that the married woman should be recognized by law to be a full and equal partner to her husband.

Article III
Goals of HERA

Section A. Because the Equal Rights Amendment will
establish that the married woman is a partner in the
family enterprise; because it will remove a married
woman from the legal mercy of her husband, and
assure her of equal justice under the law; and because
it will serve to raise the legal status of the homemaker
and strengthen the family unit: Our primary goal shall
be ratification of the Equal Rights Amendment.

1. In this regard we are committed to establishing a
   membership of individuals who favor ratification of
   the Equal Rights Amendment and support our
   goals in order to demonstrate to lawmakers and the
   general public that homemakers do want and need
   the Equal Rights Amendment.
2. In unratified states to actively work toward
   ratification through lobbying and educational
   efforts, and to support efforts to elect candidates
   who support the Equal Rights Amendment.
3. In ratified states to actively participate in lobbying
   and education efforts to protect ratification; to
   keep public interest in the amendment alive; and
   to support the efforts of unratified states.

Section B. To promote full and equal partnership under
the law for homemakers.

Section C. To promote recognition, in government, in
business, and in all areas of society, of the importance
of work done in the home.